STAN
LEE

Comic-Book Writer and Publisher

James Robert Parish

Ferguson
An imprint of ☑ Facts On File

Stan Lee: Comic-Book Writer and Publisher

Ferguson
An imprint of Facts On File, Inc.
132 West 31st Street
New York NY 10001

Library of Congress Cataloging-in-Publication Data

Parish, James Robert.
    Stan Lee : comic-book writer and publisher / James Robert Parish.
        p. cm.
    Includes index.
    ISBN 0-8160-5831-8 (hc : alk. paper)
    1. Lee, Stan. 2. Cartoonists—United States—Biography. 3. Publishers and publishing—United States—Biography. I.Title.
    PN6727.L39Z86 2006
    741.5′092—dc22   2005006438

Ferguson books are available at special discounts when purchased in bulk quantities for businesses, associations, institutions, or sales promotions. Please call our Special Sales Department in New York at (212) 967-8800 or (800) 322-8755.

You can find Ferguson on the World Wide Web at http://www.fergpubco.com

Text design by David Strelecky

Pages 98–112 adapted from Ferguson's *Encyclopedia of Careers and Vocational Guidance*

Printed in the United States of America

MP Hermitage 10 9 8 7 6 5 4 3 2 1

This book is printed on acid-free paper.

CONTENTS

1

A MARVELOUS GUY

In May 2002 the live-action film *Spider-Man* burst onto 3,615 North American movie screens. Within months the film would make more than $800 million. The film led to the successful sequel *Spider-Man 2* (2004) and plans for *Spider-Man 3* (2007), a wide array of *Spider-Man* clothes and toys, and other products. The huge success of the film also proved what Spider-Man's creator, Stan Lee, had been insisting upon for decades: The world has an enduring fascination with superheroes. Back in the early 1960s, Lee co-created some of the most famous and extraordinary comic-book characters, including Spider-Man, The Fantastic Four, The Hulk, Thor, Iron Man, Daredevil, Dr. Strange, and many others. By then Lee had already spent more than 20 years in the comic-book industry as an editor, writer, and art director at one of the industry's prime publishers, Timely (later Marvel) Comics.

The characters Lee created were unlike any that comic-book readers had ever seen. The Fantastic Four, for example, who first appeared in 1961, were different from traditional costumed superheroes such as Superman, Batman, and Wonder Woman. Whereas these other heroes were extremely well-adjusted and had few personal problems, Lee's Fantastic Four had human flaws. Readers could easily identify with this new breed of crusaders who boasted fabulous crime-fighting superpowers, but who were often weighed down with personal problems that distracted them from protecting the public. Almost overnight, Lee's innovative idea of presenting superheroes with failings boosted the sagging comic-book industry and helped bring about its "Silver Age" of success. As comic-book historian Robert Harvey pointed out in *The Art of the Comic Book: An Aesthetic History* (1996): "Nearly all modern superhero comics have drawn and continue to draw on the first 80 or so issues of The Fantastic Four for inspiration and material."

Over the next several years, Lee turned out a wide assortment of popular superhero comic books. Lee collaborated with several talented artists who illustrated his concepts within the comic-book panels (the individual boxes that frame the drawings of each story-line step). It was Lee, however, who dreamed up the array of amazingly

Stan Lee is the creator of Spider-Man and other famous comic-book characters. (Landov)

colorful personalities who inhabited these comic books, and it was he who—in the initial years—provided all of the dialogue.

Creating His Own Universe

In the 1960s Stan Lee created the characters that would make up the "Marvel Universe." In that world, heroes such as Spider-Man protected New York City and other metropolises from sinister forces bent on world domination.

Not content to rest on his laurels, Lee (known to his fans as "Stan the Man" and "Mr. Marvel") went on to become publisher of Marvel Comics in 1972. Still later, he became the firm's key spokesperson and goodwill ambassador—a post he actively continued for many years. Having begun in the business in 1940, over the decades Lee experienced the industry's many financial ups and downs and shifting trends. Despite the swings in popularity and changing fortunes of the comic-book profession, Lee has always remained highly enthusiastic about the medium through which he captured the imagination of generations.

From his beginnings in the comic-book field right through his professional heyday in the 1960s and thereafter, Stan Lee had one guiding principle: "I tried to write stories that would interest me. I'd say, what would I like to read? Then I'd try to write them clearly enough so that a youngster could enjoy and appreciate and understand the story, and I tried to write them intelligently enough so that an older person would enjoy it too." He adds, "I know what I like, and I can't believe I'm so unique. If I could write a story that really pleases me, there must be millions of people who have the same taste I do. So if I like it, there'll be a lot of other people who like it. And I've always used that rule."

2

A LOVER OF LITERATURE

Stanley Martin Lieber was born in New York on December 28, 1922, the first child of Jack and Celia (Solomon) Lieber. His parents were Jewish-Romanian immigrants. Jack worked as a dress cutter in the city's garment industry. When the Great Depression choked the U.S. economy in the late 1920s, Jack lost his job and could find no new employment. The family was forced to move from their comfortable Manhattan apartment to a cramped little place in the Bronx.

In these tiny new quarters Stanley had to sleep in the living room. This did not bother him as much as the fact that the family's new apartment looked out on the side of another building. As the future celebrity recalled, "My dream was to one day be rich enough to have an apartment that faced the street." When Stanley was eight, his second and only sibling, Larry, was born. Because there was such an age gap between the brothers, they were not close in their younger years. But later in life they would work side by side in the comic-book industry.

During Stanley's early years, his parents constantly argued—usually over money matters. Despite Jack's best efforts, the bright man was unable to find steady employment. As a result the family often had to rely on financial help from Celia's sisters, who were weathering the Depression better than the Liebers. This situation was humiliating for Jack, and he channeled some of his frustration into his relationship with his sons. In contrast, Celia was warm and encouraging to her children.

To escape the household arguments and the general gloom of the Depression, young Stanley found great pleasure in reading. He graduated from reading the Hardy Boys adventures and the works of Mark Twain (author of, among others, *The Adventures of Tom Sawyer* and *The Adventures of Huckleberry Finn*), Edgar Rice Burroughs (the creator of Tarzan), and Sir Arthur Conan Doyle (the author of the Sherlock Holmes detective tales) to reading Shakespeare before he was 10 years old. He would later remember, "I didn't understand a lot of it in those days but I loved the words. I loved the rhythms of the words." He often read books to his adoring mother and also enjoyed reading the newspaper comic strips of the era, especially "Krazy Kat" and "They'll Do It Every Time."

Besides his growing love of literature, Stanley loved to scribble "little illustrated stories to amuse myself. I would draw a straight horizontal line for the horizon and then add stick figures above it, around which I built simple stories and plot lines. I was, without knowing it, creating my first comicbooks. This was a make-believe world I loved because I could retreat to it from the outside—particularly from school."

Stanley also loved going to the movies when he could scrape together the pennies for admission. There he reveled in the big-screen westerns, detective stories, and swashbuckling heroes of the day. "There on the screen were worlds that dazzled my mind," he says, "worlds of magic and wonder, worlds which I longed to inhabit, if only in my imagination." Then too, Stanley was excited by the animated cartoon short subjects he saw, especially the work of Walt Disney and his most famous cartoon creation, Mickey Mouse. In fact, Stanley was so inspired by Disney's animation output that it prompted the future comic-book king to say, "I admired him so when I was a kid. I probably created many more characters, but he created an empire. I'm not an empire creator."

Stanley also loved when his family would gather, especially on Sunday evenings, to listen to popular radio programs of the day, especially comedians such as Eddie Cantor, Jack Benny, and Fred Allen.

One of the biggest moments of young Stanley's childhood occurred when his family scraped together enough money to buy him a two-wheeler bicycle. This gift meant a tremendous amount to him: "When I rode it, in my imagination I was a mighty knight atop a noble steed. That bike was my best friend because it gave me a feeling of freedom. So what if our family didn't have a car. I finally had wheels. I could ride all over the city, go wherever I pleased. No kid ever loved a bike more than I loved mine."

The Responsible Young Man

As the Depression continued in the 1930s, Jack Lieber still had great difficulty finding steady employment and would take whatever temporary jobs he could to help the family survive. Stanley was well aware of his father's unsuccessful efforts at being the family's chief breadwinner. Years later Stanley would recall, "I always felt tremendous pity for him, because it must be a terrible feeling to be a man and not be bringing in the money that is needed for your family." Mr. Lieber's plight left a great impression on the youth, who vowed that when he grew to adulthood, he would always find ways to take care of his family so their lives would not be as stressful as his had been.

When Stanley was 13 he went through his Bar Mitzvah, a Jewish religious ceremony that signified that he had passed from childhood into adulthood. Now no longer considered a boy, Stanley took on part-time jobs so he could contribute to the household income. Among several other positions, Stanley was a delivery boy who brought sandwiches to office workers and worked as an usher at the Rivoli Theater in midtown Manhattan. One of his greatest memories of working at this movie palace was the time that Eleanor Roosevelt, then the first lady of the United States, attended a showing at the theater, accompanied by several secret service men. She chose to be seated in Stan's aisle. As he proudly walked her to her seat, he tripped over someone's outstretched legs. It was the kindly first lady who helped the embarrassed youth to his feet.

For a brief time, Stanley was employed by a news service. There he assisted in preparing obituaries of celebrated individuals so that when they died their write-ups could be quickly updated and provided to member newspapers. Stanley found this task too depressing and soon quit. His other jobs included writing public relations materials for a Jewish hospital based in Denver. Then, for a time, the ambitious young man was employed by the U.S. government's Works Progress Administration (WPA). He was assigned to the Federal Theater, which provided work for unemployed members of the stage profession. Although Stanley labored only briefly for the WPA by helping with the production of a few plays, it instilled in him a great affection for acting. (In later years, he gleefully accepted small roles in feature films and was active on the college lecture circuit.)

As Stanley became a successful wage earner, his mother lavished even more love on him. She was forever holding him up as an example to brother Larry, urging the much younger boy to try be more like Stanley. Celia Lieber would say to Larry, "Why don't you read books the way your brother does and be literate and be like Stan?" This constant praising of Stanley—at Larry's expense—widened the gulf between the two siblings. The duo never spent much time together until later in life. By then, too many lost years had passed between the pair and they were never able to build a really close bond.

Classroom Heroes

By the mid-1930s Stanley was attending DeWitt Clinton High School, a very crowded all-boys school in the Bronx. Ambitious and bright, Stanley had already skipped grades. He was also prodded along by his mother, who hoped that he could graduate earlier than normal and obtain a full-time job to help support the family.

Often the youngest pupil in his class, Stanley experienced a lot of peer pressure as a teenager and generally felt like an outsider. Helping to smooth out these difficult years was his admiration for one of his teachers, Leon B. Ginsberg Jr. Stanley has said, "He would entertain the class with humorous and exciting stories to illustrate teaching points. It was Mr. Ginsberg who first made me realize that learning could be fun, that it was easier to reach people, to hold their attention, to get points across, with humor than any other way. It was a lesson I never forgot, a lesson I've tried to apply to everything I do." (Using humor to capture an audience's attention would prove to be very useful when, later in life, Stan frequently lectured at colleges about the comic-book industry.)

Another inspiration for Stanley in this period was newspaper correspondent Floyd Gibbons, who, years earlier, had daringly tracked, met, rode with, and written about Mexican revolutionary Pancho Villa. Later Gibbons served courageously in World War I and thereafter returned to the United States and wrote a popular newspaper column. Gibbons was one of Stanley's heroes, and the teenager was thrilled when the journalist actually answered a fan letter he had written him.

It might have been that brush with the professional world of writing that inspired Stanley to enter a contest sponsored by the *New York Herald-Tribune*. Each week the newspaper picked a winner from among the high school students who sent in their short accounts of what they considered "The Best News of the Week." On one occasion, Stanley won seventh place (with a $2.50 prize). Another time he received an honorable mention in the *Herald-Tribune* competition. Although he never won the competition, achieving some recognition encouraged Stanley to pursue the creative lines that would lead to his future career.

Another of Stanley's idols was a fellow student at DeWitt Clinton High, John J. McKenna Jr., who was a few grades ahead of Stanley and became remarkable to him for his powers of persuasion. John was a sales representative for the *New York Times* and would come into various classrooms to urge the students to subscribe to this newspaper, providing a host of reasons to do so. The older boy's sales knack and ease in addressing an audience made a strong impression on Stanley: "He spoke for about ten full minutes, looking his audience straight in the eye, never once fumbling or losing the attention of the class. I was terribly impressed by the smooth, easygoing way he made his pitch and the way he managed to hold the interest of the students while talking about a subject that normally would bore the pants off them." According to Stan, "I decided that I wanted to be able to speak that way, to be able to hold the attention of an audience the way he did." Ironically, the two students never met, but John McKenna had a strong influence on the younger man's life. In fact, when Stanley was a senior he too sold newspaper subscriptions to the *Herald-Tribune* to fellow students.

Moving into the Real World

During his high school years, the always busy Stanley found time between his class work and his part-time jobs to participate in extracurricular activities at DeWitt Clinton. He was a member of the debating club, the French club, the ping-pong group, and the chess club. In addition, Stanley participated in the (pre-) law society; at one point he wanted to become an attorney after seeing the profession glamorously depicted in motion picture dramas. He was also a staff worker on the school's *Magpie* magazine, where he handled publicity but wrote no stories. At school Stanley was nicknamed "Gabby" for his habit of endless chatting. In his yearbook, Stanley wrote that his life's goal was to "Reach the Top—and STAY There." He also noted in his school almanac that he intended to "Join the navy, so the world can see me!"

After graduating high school in 1939, Stanley did not have the option of attending college. He always regretted not being a part of the campus life he had seen in the movies. However, he was responsible enough to accept that he now had to help support his family. One of the recent graduate's first jobs was working for a trouser manufacturer in New York's garment district. Stanley became an errand boy for the firm's many salesmen. He found the work exhausting and mortifying, especially hating when they would shout out "Boy!" and he had to jump to the salesmen's latest bidding. A few weeks later—just before Christmas—there was a cutback at the firm. Because Stanley was the newest employee, they fired him, even though he had worked much harder and more effectively than another office boy who joined the company a month before and was kept on at the firm. Stanley viewed the termination with a sigh of relief and also with a bit of rebellion. Before he departed the despised job he overturned a few of the tightly packed inventory containers that he had spent so much time and effort organizing.

At this crucial time Stan's uncle Robbie Solomon came up with an employment suggestion for his nephew. Robbie Solomon was employed at Timely Publications, a firm owned and operated by Martin Goodman, who happened to be another member—by marriage—of the Lieber-Solomon family. Stanley was told there might be a job for him at the publishing company's cramped Manhattan office.

At Timely, Stanley was interviewed by Joe Simon, the company's editor, and was introduced to Jack Kirby, the art director. Because the small firm was experiencing a boost in popularity as a result of its expanding line of comic books, Simon and Kirby needed an assistant. Stan was hired to be their gofer for $8 weekly. Not sure what the future would entail at Timely, nevertheless, Stan quickly accepted the position. Little did he know it was the beginning of his lifetime career.

3

EXCITING NEW VISTAS

When teenaged Stanley Lieber first learned of a job opening at Timely Publications, he imagined that he would be working in the world of magazines—particularly in the firm's established line of exciting pulp publications that focused on tales of romance, fantasy, crime, and the Old West. But at the point that Stanley joined Timely, it was undergoing a change in product focus. The company was now specializing in churning out comic books.

Early Comics, from Yellow Kid to Superman

The origin of comic books dates back to newspaper comic strips that first gained popularity in the United States in 1895, when Richard F. Outcault's "The Yellow Kid" appeared in the *New York World*. The huge success of this strip led to merchandise licensing, stage adaptations, and so forth, all revolving around the strip's lead character, a pushy, colorful slum youth. Because "The Yellow Kid" was so profitable, it led others to create such competing strips as "The Katzenjammer Kids," "Little Jimmy," "Barney Google," and "Toonerville Folks." These offerings appeared weekdays in newspapers around the country (usually in black-and-white art work and often in color for the weekend entries).

Meanwhile, in the early 1900s newsstands across America were filled increasingly with pulp magazines (which gained their name because they were published on low-cost, coarse pulp paper). They often featured trashy, and sometimes lurid, short fiction. Compared to more costly hardback books, pulp publications were geared to be inexpensive, quick and simple to read, and disposable. The sensational pulp stories—including such standout examples as the jungle adventures of Tarzan of the Apes and the outer space exploits of Buck Rogers— developed quite a strong public following, especially in the post-World War I period of the 1920s and early 1930s.

After pulp fiction magazines became an established reading tradition, a new twist came along in 1933. Harry Wildenberg and Max C. Gaines, who worked for the Eastern Color Printing Company, came up with the idea of a 32-page booklet that would reprint Sunday comic strips in splashy colors. (There had been some earlier efforts to reprint comic strips in black and white editions, but they lacked the new convenient format or newsstand distribution to be very successful.) When this first offering—entitled *Funnies on Parade*—was sold to Proctor & Gamble to be used as a promotional giveaway, it was an instant hit. Wildenberg and Gaines began to sell other such comic reprint collections on the nation's newsstands at a reasonable 10-cent price tag.

By 1935 Major Malcolm Wheeler-Nicholson, a one-time U.S. cavalry officer and a previous writer of pulp stories, entered the expanding field. He came up with the notion of publishing original comic strips in several panels that made up a short story-length episode. His initial publication was *New Fun Comics,* an anthology of assorted comic strip narratives featuring entries in the humor, Western, and adventure veins. Within the next year, Harry Chesler set up a shop that was a factory-like assembly line for churning out comic books for such clients as Wheeler-Nicholson and such others as Centaur, Fawcett, and MLJ. In 1937 Wheeler-Nicholson formed Detective Comics Inc. (the firm that later changed its name to DC Comics) with two partners, Harry Donnerfield and Jack Liebowitz. The latter two soon bought out the financially strapped Wheeler-Nicholson and, in 1938, published a new comic book, *Action Comics #1*. This entry featured a man of steel who strode and flew about in his red-and-blue costume, helping people in distress. He was known as Superman.

The huge success of the Action Comics *character Superman prompted national interest in the comic-book field.* (Associated Press)

The ongoing adventures of the amazing Superman proved so popular with readers that, before long, each monthly issue of *Action Comics* was selling over 1.25 million copies. (A similar triumph was enjoyed by Detective Comics' next big comic-book property, *Batman*, another fantastic costumed avenger of wrong who boasted a sidekick, Robin. Like Superman, Batman and Robin had secret real-life identities.) These major successes induced several other businessmen to rush into the profitable field. Within a few years there were nearly 170 different comic-book entries being published on a frequent basis. By now there was an established tradition that comic-book artists and writers were paid a page rate (typically around $10 per page) and that ownership of the characters and stories belonged to the publishers (who made and kept all the big profits).

Martin Goodman and Timely Publications

Back in 1932, Martin Goodman, then 22 years old, first became involved in the pulp magazine industry. He launched his enterprise with several Western-themed entries such as *Quick Trigger Western Novel*. Goodman's firm took careful note of each new trend in pulp magazines. As a new genre became popular with the buying public, Martin would immediately order his staff to turn out rip-off entries in the same category to take advantage of the current craze. Goodman utilized a variety of company names for his array of product, one of them being Timely.

By the late 1930s Goodman's publishing operation was going through a financial slump, as was much of the pulp magazine industry. He was approached by Frank Torpey, who represented a comic-book factory (which sold its product to interested buyers for them to market to the public). The salesman persuaded Goodman to hire Torpey's employer, Funnies Inc., to produce a fresh line of comic books to be published by Timely. Wanting to take advantage of the superhero fad in the business, Goodman's first offering, *Marvel Comics #1*, was an anthology of comic-strip tales highlighting its own lineup of superheroes. One of these strip episodes featured the Human Torch, whose spectacular metallic body generated such heat it could set targets ablaze. Another story focused on the Sub-Mariner, whose extraordinary powers came from the mysterious ocean deep.

When the first *Marvel* issue sold well, Goodman continued in the same publishing vein. He changed the name of his flagship entry to *Marvel Mystery Comics* and added more titles to his product line (e.g., *Daring Mystery Comics*), which showcased such superhuman figures as Flexo the Rubber Man. But it was Timely's Sub-Mariner and the Human Torch that proved most successful. Before long, each was highlighted in its own series of comic books. All these comic-book ventures were published under the Timely label and became Goodman's major effort as the pulp magazine industry continued its downward slide.

To handle his fast-growing comic-book line, Martin Goodman hired Joe Simon, then in his mid-20s and already freelancing for Timely, to become the company's editor. Another freelance artist, Jack Kirby, a collaborator and friend of Simon, came aboard Timely to be its staff artist/art director. The two new employees experimented with a variety of fresh superhero characters (e.g., the Vision) before coming up in late 1940 with Captain America. This phenomenal figure was dedicated to fighting the Nazi Germany enemy that was fast overrunning Europe and threatening to draw the United States into World War II. This patriotic superhero made his debut in *Captain America Comics #1.* It was so well received by comic-book buyers that Goodman decided to make the profitable property a monthly publication. Because Simon and Kirby were already overextended in their creative efforts, they begged their boss to hire an assistant.

The new worker brought into the Timely fold was Stanley Lieber, a cousin of Jean Goodman, Martin's wife.

The New Kid on the Block

Stanley began working at Timely in the fall of 1940. The 17-year old did a variety of odd jobs, from making coffee, sweeping the floor, and keeping the artists' ink bottles filled to erasing the pencil sketch lines that lay beneath the finished drawings. Stanley was one of a dozen individuals—mostly relatives—who labored in-house at Timely. A large percentage of the talent the firm used consisted of freelance artists and writers paid by the page for their work.

Almost from the start, it was clear to others at Timely that young Stanley was a go-getter and a very quick learner. Stanley was at the company only for a week before boldly asking for a raise. While his brazen request was being considered, Simon gave the ambitious new worker an additional task. At the time, each published comic book contained two pages or so of pure text, which were added merely to qualify the publication for less expensive mailing rates. Stanley was told to write one of these slapped-together pieces, which buyers rarely read. Using the type of language he had seen in pulp magazines, Stanley quickly concocted 26 paragraphs of haphazard writing, which he entitled "Captain America Foils the Traitor's Revenge." The brief story ran in the May 1941 issue of *Captain America Comics*.

Stanley signed his debut piece with the pseudonym Stan Lee. It was common practice in the pulp magazine/comic-book business for writers and artists to use pen names because they often worked for several rival publications at the same time or had a following or set of characters in another genre and did not wish to confuse their fans. Then too, the young writer also had high hopes of one day writing important novels and did not want to have his real name associated with the disreputable world of comic books. (In actuality, Stanley had first used the pen name Stan Lee when he was at DeWitt Clinton High School. He had scrawled "Stan Lee is God" on the ceiling of a room used for extracurricular activities.)

Having made his unspectacular entrance into the comic-book field, Stan's next step was to provide the script for an actual comic-book adventure. In *Captain America Comics #5* (which had a cover date of August 1941), Stan contributed the script for "Headline Hunter, Foreign Correspondent." He also took on the "Father Time" series, a Timely entry that revolved around a character—costumed, of course—who dealt justice with the aid of a lethal scythe. Because Stan wanted the world to know that these were his creative efforts, the opening panel (called the *splash panel*) would read "Story by Stan Lee."

As Timely grew increasingly busy in 1941 with its expanding line of successful comic books, Stan found himself writing a larger number of scripts. Written quickly (often in a day or an evening) for an undemanding market, they were not great prose, but Stan's dialogue balloons for the comic-book panels showed his enthusiasm and growing sense of humor as he gained confidence in his new trade.

Jumping Ahead

During 1941, Joe Simon and Jack Kirby (Timely's editor and art director, respectively) became more and more unhappy at Timely. Overworked and frustrated by the demands and controls of Martin Goodman, they began to explore professional options elsewhere. The pair escalated their efforts when they came to believe that Goodman was not properly paying them their percentage of profits—part of their newer agreement with the hard-nosed firm—on the successful comics they had created. In this period, the dissatisfied duo were wooed by DC Comics and began negotiating to work on the side for Timely's rival. Somehow the information was leaked to Martin Goodman. In a burst of anger, he fired his two key employees.

With Simon and Kirby suddenly gone, Goodman immediately promoted Stan to editorial director of the thriving firm. He made clear to Stan that this was a temporary measure until he could find a full-time, experienced professional to take over the demanding post. Meanwhile, the publisher filled the talent gap by hiring cartoonist Al Avison and another young artist, Syd Shores, to handle the penciling and inking/art director chores, respectively, at Timely.

Stan was incredibly young to hold such a senior position at the firm. As he would recount in his memoir, *Excelsior!*

The Amazing Life of Stan Lee (written with George Mair), "In some ways, I was embarrassed to let visitors to the office know that I was the editor because they might think we weren't a serious business if an eighteen-year-old kid was running the shop. Sometimes I'd be in the reception room and some grown-up would come in and see me sitting there in my sneakers and sweatshirt, and say, 'Hey, kid, where can I find Mr. Lee?' It would always embarrass me, because I knew he himself would be embarrassed if I said, 'I'm Mr. Lee.' So instead, I'd say, 'Just a minute, sir, I'll tell him you're here.' Then I'd run out and call the receptionist, 'Tell him Mr. Lee is gone for the day.' "

By 1942, Goodman still had not found a permanent replacement for Stan, who continued in his high-pressure position, in which he ably supervised the massive flow of work from the in-house and freelance artists and writers. He had to ensure that the work was coordinated properly and delivered to the printers on specified deadlines to avoid substantial financial penalties. In addition, Stan continued to script an increasing number of the comic books turned out by Timely. (Besides his editorial salary, Stan was being paid on a per-page basis for his comic-book scripting chores. Because of the speed with which he created and wrote these scripts—geared to the reading abilities and tastes of the young—he was making a tidy extra income.) To make even more efficient use of his precious time, hyperactive Stan began phoning some of the outside artists to dictate the scripts for the comic they were working on. Typically, he would tell the artist, "Take it to the ultimate point. Don't give me the in-between stuff." With that, lightning-fast Lee turned his attention to the next immediate task on his crowded agenda.

Looking back on his informal entry into, and quick rise within, the booming comic-book field, Stan has said that he learned all the elements of his craft on the job. He has acknowledged that part of his career education came from studying the work of professionals from competing firms to gain the wisdom of their expertise of the business. According to Stan, "Nobody sat down and told anyone how to do it. Nobody had any respect for comics. It was the lowest rung on the creative totem pole." As he only half-chidingly remarked, at that time publishers of comic books were content with hiring "anybody who could put two words together and work cheap enough."

Stan soon became an expert in his administrative/editorial/writing position of editorial director, which was still considered a temporary placement. Other, more senior employees quickly learned to accept his input and orders and came to rely on his quick decisions, which were based on the wishes of publisher Martin Goodman. For example, when Goodman determined that his competitors were making more money from humorous animal tale comic books than from superhero comics, Timely began rolling out barnyard comic books. Thus came *Joker Comics #1* and the conversion of the *Daring Mystery* comic-book into *Comedy Comics*. While still whipping together such staples as the daring exploits of brave Captain America and the Destroyer, Stan began scripting the escapades of new animal characters such as Ziggy Pig, Little Lester, and Silly Seal.

In the process of writing funny animal antics, Stan came to several useful conclusions: "Comedy is one of the highest forms of entertainment." He believed that humor should always flow from the characters. "Everything is characterization. I'm not turned on by just jokes. It's got to mean something."

Helping Uncle Sam

On December 7, 1941, Japan made a surprise attack on a U.S. military base in Pearl Harbor, Hawaii, and the United States officially entered World War II. Immediately, thousands of patriotic men rushed to enlist in the armed forces, while many others were soon drafted into service. Soon Stan felt the urge to serve his country in the battlefield abroad. His employer, however, kept insisting that Stan was doing his bit for the country by turning out comic-book adventures, which were so beloved by the young men in the armed services. But as the fall of 1942 arrived, Stan became convinced that he too must join the military to be "a hero like [movie stars] Errol Flynn . . . or John Wayne."

Not yet 20 years old, Stan was excited at the potential great adventures that lay ahead of him as a new enlistee in the army. Although fearful of the actual combat he would face, Stan tried to overcome his anxiety. He remembers, "I used to go to penny arcades in New York and shoot those little guns and win prizes all the time—I figured I was a shoo-in to handle real guns."

Before becoming a soldier, Stan found a replacement to take over his many tasks at Timely. He turned to a friend, Vince Fago, an artist who had been working on the company's humorous animal comics, to take over his position.

Saying his goodbyes at work and to his family at home, Stan Lee set out to fight America's real-life enemies.

4

THE TYPEWRITER WARRIOR

In 1942 Stan Lee reported to the U.S. Army base at Fort Monmouth, New Jersey, for basic training. After enduring the standard toughening-up process, the new recruit was assigned to guard duty on the nearby New Jersey shore. This relatively safe assignment continued for some days before he was given a brand new set of orders. He learned he had been given the classification of playwright (one of nine such individuals in the whole U.S. Army at the time). As such he was assigned to the Signal Corps, the Army's communications group. He was commanded to report to Astoria, New York, where the military had taken over a former film studio lot for their operations. In his new job, Stan was one of the team responsible for writing—and illustrating—training manuals used to teach new enlisted men the various skills and information they needed to survive their tours of military duty. He also helped with the scripts for military training films used for the same purposes.

In his new position, Stan worked on a variety of publications. He prepared payroll manuals that would help speed up the accounting processes through which soldiers receive their monthly pay. To give the booklets a humorous touch—which he felt would make the dry reading more appealing—Stan created a character called Fiscal Freddy. He also created a catchy poster that encouraged lowering the risk of sexually transmitted diseases. In addition, Stan composed a marching song to be utilized by the Army's finance department.

As he had also proved during his time at Timely, in his Army communications position Stan proved to be a quick learner with a flair for writing and humor. Later, when Stan was reassigned and based at Duke University in North Carolina—where many military units were then quartered—he finally got his first car: a secondhand 1936 Plymouth. By now he was used to his comparatively easy wartime duties and felt it was time to take on more responsibility on behalf of his country. He wanted to apply for officers' candidate school, but his commanding officer refused the request. (The superior officer did not wish to lose Stan's useful talents.) Still further into World

War II, Stan was transferred to Fort Benjamin Harrison in Indiana, where he pursued the same line of duties.

The Moonlighter

While Stan—as well as many other comic-book artists and writers—was serving his country in World War II, the comic-book industry was booming. By 1943 more than 25 million comic books were being sold monthly. Enjoying high profits, Martin Goodman moved Timely Publications to roomier headquarters on the 14th floor of the Empire State Building. Needing a steady flow of workers, Goodman did not rely only on those talents exempted or rejected from military duty. He also counted upon the freelance services of seasoned industry personnel who were in the armed forces but whose stateside assignments allowed them the opportunity to work for Timely.

One of these moonlighters was Stan Lee. He would spend the late evening hours, and whatever spare weekend time he could find, fulfilling the writing tasks offered by his old boss. Goodman set up a system in which he would send a letter to Stan specifying the latest comic-book writing assignments and the deadlines involved. (One of these comic-book writing assignments was for a comic-strip entitled "Super Soldier," which took a satirical look at army life. Stan signed that particular piece "Pfc. Stan Lee.") Having completed the assignment, Stan would then mail the hastily assembled work back to Goodman who, in turn, sent Stan a check for his latest efforts. Sometimes on a weekend when he was off-duty for a longer stretch, Stan would rent a room at a nearby hotel and spend hours grinding out projects for Goodman. On a highly productive weekend, Stan would earn about $500, terrific pocket money in the 1940s.

One week Stan did not receive his usual correspondence from the always punctual Goodman, and he was puzzled. The next day, Saturday, Stan happened to walk by the mail room and spotted a letter in the "L" cubbyhole. He could see from the envelope that it was from Timely. Not wanting to miss out on the assignment and the future paycheck, Stan went to the company clerk and explained he had spotted a letter in the locked mail room that was for him and requested to retrieve it. Stan was brusquely informed that the mailroom was closed on weekends and that was that. Being rambunctious and tired of petty rules in the military, Stan found a screwdriver and unscrewed the lock on the mailroom door. After grabbing his envelope, he reinstated the lock. That accomplished, he fulfilled his job for Timely and mailed it off. Once again, he had managed to meet his deadline. All was well—or so he thought. His commanding officer had somehow discovered the break in and was determined to punish his unruly subordinate. But Stan's talents were considered so valuable that other officers at the base interceded on his behalf, and Stan avoided punishment—which could have meant time in the stockade.

As World War II finally came to a close in 1945, servicemen around the globe were making plans for what they would do once back in civilian life. One of Stan's service pals, Lt. Harry Stonehill, urged his Army buddy not to return to the childish world of comic books. This former Chicago businessman suggested that his friend join him in the Philippines when they were discharged. Stonehill already had a plan to start marketing Christmas cards in that tropical country. Stan appreciated the unusual offer but thought his chum's plan was far too wild and impractical. As it turned out, Stonehill did quite well in his enterprise in the Philippines and went on to become one of that nation's wealthiest men. Stan became both impressed by his friend's business skills and furious with himself for passing up such a golden opportunity to become extremely rich. But as time would tell, Stan's determination and talents would enable him to reap his own rewards.

The Happy Civilian

As of September 29, 1945, Sgt. Stanley M. Lieber received an honorable discharge from the U.S. Army. He boasted a good conduct medal for his nearly three years serving his country at bases around the United States. Once back in New York City, he treated himself to booking a two-room suite at a nice hotel, which became his new civilian residence.

There was no problem in Stan returning to Timely Publications in his old position now that he was released from military service. Rather than become Stan's assistant, Vince Fago, who had been filling in while Stan was in the military, quietly surrendered his editorship of the comic books and returned to being a freelance artist within the industry.

After the war, business was booming for Timely and the whole comic-book industry. Although superhero comics were still popular, they had lost their novelty and edge through overexposure, especially from the many low-caliber ripoffs that filled the newsstand racks. Now the latest hot trends in the ever-changing comic-book business were romance tales, crime dramas, Western adventures, and women's stories.

As with the humorous animal tales, Timely was never the innovator of these genre crazes but followed in the paths of its adventurous competitors, hoping to jump into a successful niche before it became too oversaturated. Thus Stan was in charge of editing, writing, and getting to publication not only the tried and true entries but new comics for women, such as *Tessie the Typist, Hedy of Hol-*

lywood, and *Millie the Model*. Another gimmick that Timely tried—copying their comic-book rivals—was combining several of their lead superheroes into one big slam-bang comic-book publication. Thus 1946's *The All Winners Squad* presented the joint adventures of the Human Torch, Sub-Mariner, Miss America, the Whizzer, and Captain America. Readers' tastes being unpredictable, however, these innovative combinations of superheroes did not grab their attention and were dropped after two issues.

Later, Timely had more success with the crime category, turning out such titles as *Crime Cases*, *True Complete Mystery*, and *Casey, Crime Photographer*. Western comic books, which included Timely's sagebrush superhero the Black Rider, experienced a period of popularity. Then war-themed comics took the spotlight, and Timely churned out such books as *Combat Kelly*, *Battle Brady*, and *Battle Comics*. As Goodman rapidly switched from genre to genre to make fresh stabs at grabbing readers' attention, he dropped quickly those entries that did not sell. And all the while, workaholic Stan kept pace with his Goodman's latest orders.

Questioning His Career

Although Stan was happy to have full-time work in a field in which he was fast becoming an authority, he still had lofty artistic dreams. He still wanted to write the great

American novel or become a successful screenwriter or a Broadway playwright. Despite his great dreams, they never seemed to translate into reality or even into a strong creative effort on his part. He told himself he was too busy with the high-pressure job of being the editorial director of a highly successful comic-book firm. Nevertheless, he still had not come to terms with his profession and how the public then viewed the comic-book field.

As time passed, Stan would frequently recount how, in those post-World War II years, he would be at a social gathering and the inevitable would happen. Someone would ask him the question: "What do you do for a living?" Since many people considered comic books to be an industry of hacks looking to make a quick dollar, Stan would vaguely reply that he was a writer. Typically, the other person would want more information, and Stan would mumble that he wrote "Stories for young people." If the questioner would persist and push Stan for more particulars, he would then blurt out, "I write comic books." According to Stan, that would be the moment the person would lose interest and quickly drift away.

During this period of questioning his career, Stan was pleased when *Writer's Digest* magazine asked him to compose a feature article for their November 1947 issue. His lead piece was "There's Money in Comics," and the publication placed his photograph (showing Stan in a distinguished pose smoking a pipe) on the issue's cover. In the article, Stan set forth principles for aspiring comic-book writers. These guidelines included "Have a Provocative Beginning," "Use Smooth Continuity from Panel to Panel," "Concentrate on Realistic Dialogue Which Leads to Good Characterization," "Maintain Suspense Throughout," and finally, "Provide a Satisfying Ending."

That same year, Stan used his "spare" time to turn out *The Secrets Behind the Comics*. Detailing how comic books were produced, the small publication was structured in comic-book format and boasted illustrations by several Timely freelancers (including Ken Bald). Stan sold the book for $1 from his apartment headquarters.

Finding His Soul Mate

When he wasn't working, Stan enjoyed an active and care-free social life. That all changed, however, in 1947. One day Stan was supposed to be fixed up with a model named Betty. When he arrived to pick up his date, he was met at the apartment door by the young woman's roommate. To Stan's amazement, this pretty, blue-eyed redhead closely resembled the face of his ideal woman that he had been doodling on scrap paper since his teenaged years. The real-life female was Joan Clayton Boocock, a hat model. She was from Newcastle-on-Tyne, England. She had met her first husband at the end of World War II. After knowing him for only 24 hours, she had married the U.S. soldier. They soon moved to New York City. Now, a year later, her marriage was falling apart. Stan was fascinated with Joan, and she with him.

Soon the two were very much in love with one another and embarked on a whirlwind romance. Later, Joan announced that she was soon going to Reno, Nevada, to obtain a divorce. The laws of that state required a six-week residency for the party seeking to terminate the marriage. Joan was gone for five weeks when Lee suddenly decided he would fly out to join his beloved. Stan was at her side the day she went to court to receive her divorce. As soon as the divorce papers were signed, Stan turned to the judge and asked him to marry him and Joan. So on December 5, 1947—a few weeks before Stan's 25th birthday—he became a married man.

The newlyweds moved into a brownstone building in Manhattan. They enjoyed domestic life in their small apartment. While Joan decorated their new home, Stan continued his chores at Timely, where the in-house and freelance staff was growing. Stan now had two editors working under his direction. Recalling this period of high productivity but few original ideas at Timely, Stan rationalized, "I was just doing what my publisher asked me to do. Being young, I enjoyed the feeling of importance of being editor and art director and head writer." In retrospect he realized, "It never occurred to me that what I was doing wasn't all that great."

Meanwhile, Joan abandoned her modeling career and aspirations of becoming an actress to be a housewife. Soon the couple had a new member living in their household. When Stan's mother died, Stan's 16-year-old brother, Larry, who felt closer to his brother than to his father,

Joan and Stan Lee in 2004 (Getty Images)

moved in with Stan and Joan. Finding that the tight quarters were too cramped for three, they moved to Hewlett Harbor in Long Island, where they took up residence in a remodeled carriage house in a fancy neighborhood. The relatively well-to-do locals did not know what to make of the newcomers, especially Stan, who worked for those "silly little magazines for little children."

In April 1950 the Lees became parents of a baby girl whom they named Joan Celia. Overjoyed at becoming parents, they looked forward to having more children. However, in 1953, the Lees' second daughter, Jan, died three days after her birth. Once over their grief, they thought of adding to their family by adopting a baby boy but eventually decided against going through the lengthy process.

Meanwhile, to spend more time with his loved ones and to cut down on the lengthy commute between Long Island and Manhattan, Stan convinced Martin Goodman to let him stay at home one (then two or more) days a week. To fulfill his comic-book writing assignments, Stan would often type his latest effort from a standing position on his terrace so he could better absorb the sun and not develop a body slouch from sitting so much in front of a typewriter. Because so many of the (freelance) artists employed by Timely lived on Long Island, they would often drop by Stan's home to pick up scripts and to discuss their next comic-book assignments.

While Stan's life was hectic (he worked nearly seven days a week), he thrived on his regimen of hard work. He was also driven to such a grueling schedule after seeing his own father struggle unsuccessfully to support his family. Stan remembered all too well the strain that lack of decent income had had on the household. As the provider, Stan was sticking to his vow to never let that happen to him or his loved ones. As a result, he worked far harder than he should have and was constantly worried that a downturn in the ever-changing comic-book industry might pull down his happy home life.

5

COMBATING THE CRUSADE AGAINST COMIC BOOKS

During the 1950s, Stan and others in the comic-book trade began to realize the great changes that the end of World War II brought to the industry. With millions of servicemen returning home after the war, the U.S. government was no longer ordering and shipping tons of comic books to the armed forces abroad. Once reestablished into civilian life, the flood of ex-G.I.s soon settled into marriage and all its accompanying domestic responsibilities. No longer did they have the time or spare money to spend on the wide assortment of comic books they had during the war years. This loss of comic-book readership kept mounting as the 1940s ended.

Also by the late 1940s, commercial television was becoming increasingly popular in the United States as TV sets became more affordable. Former comic-book buyers/readers suddenly became glued to the small screen, where they could watch entertainment for free.

Adding to the industry's problems was the fact that there were so many established and new comic books flooding the newsstands that the average reader was becoming overwhelmed with the variety of products. Many of these books seemed (and often were) a rehash of what had been published previously in one form or another. Because of the heated competition among the major publishers in the field, if a new trend (such as romance comic books) suddenly grabbed readers' interest and enjoyed a flurry of good sales, rival firms would quickly publish their own variations of the trendy subject matter. This practice weakened the success of all the entries in the field. As the popularity of one genre died down, publishers experimented with other subject formats, hoping to excite the interest of the dwindling buying public. Unfortunately, the same copycat situation occurred all over again.

A Big Threat to the Comic-Book Industry

In the United States, at one time or another, most of the creative arts have come under the investigation of public or government censorship groups. In the early 1920s, Hollywood became the focus of morality organizations who felt the movie industry went far beyond the norms of decency. Growing pressure led the panicked film industry to create its own self-censorship group, which gained power and control over the film business in the mid-1930s—a stranglehold which lasted for several decades.

The comic-book business also had its share of hard times with censorship. Going back to the early 1900s, civic groups were already protesting newspaper comic strips, which they claimed promoted unruly behavior on the part of the readers—especially children. The argument that comics had a negative moral impact was revived in the 1930s. Then it was argued that the comic-strip capers of "Dick Tracy" and "Terry and the Pirates" were far too racy for innocent youngsters.

Another serious threat to the comic-strip/comic-book business occurred in the spring of 1940, when newspaper writer Sterling North wrote the article "A National Disgrace" in the *Chicago Daily News*. This lengthy article argued that comics were helping to ruin the morality and cultural standards of school children. The piece was republished in several other newspapers and created a great impact at the time. It led to the formation of many parents groups around the nation who lobbied against the ill effects of comics. In reaction, a few publishers, such as

Parents Magazine's *True Comics* (1941), began to focus on very wholesome characters and bland story lines in their upcoming books. As World War II became a growing reality to Americans, however, the anti-comic-book campaign faded—for the time being—and things were much as before within the industry.

After World War II, censorship groups again gained strength and launched campaigns about the bad effects of most comic books on youth. In reaction to this rising tide against the comic-book business, some publishers banded together to create a self-censorship organization, the Comics Magazine Association of America (CMAA). They assured the angry protest groups that their new, sanitized product was not damaging the minds and morals of America's youth.

Watching this growing outcry for comic-book censorship, publisher Martin Goodman at Timely, which was transforming into the Marvel Comics Group, tried something different. He hired a well-known psychiatrist to monitor the quality of stories being published by Marvel. Jumping into the battle, Stan Lee wrote passionate editorials in the Timely/Marvel publications promoting the idea that the public had a constitutional right "to read what they wanted to read." In his articles, Stan lampooned Dr. Fredric Wertham, who was the author of *Seduction of the Innocent* (1954) and was considered the leading

In the 1940s comic books came under attack by censorship groups. Here children are putting their comic collections in a truck to be part of a bonfire. (Associated Press)

spokesperson in the battle to control the so-called dangers of comic books. At one point—for a spring 1953 issue of a Marvel comic book—Stan prepared a short story called "The Raving Maniac," which poked fun at the ranting of Dr. Wertham.

Despite the anti-censorship efforts of Stan and others in the industry, the attack against the comic-book industry reached new heights. In April 1954 the U.S. Senate formed a subcommittee to examine the dangers in the contents of comic books to formative minds.

This public airing on the comic-book business caused one of the leading publishers—EC Comics—to help organize the CMAA. This group established a code to control the contents of their publications. Among the rules established was one that attempted to tone down any examples of violence, especially the use of rampaging aliens (part of the then current sci-fi comic-book trend). Such guidelines made it difficult for Stan and others to present comic-book characters, plot, and dialogue in the ways they had in the past.

The Industry Fallout

As the CMAA's code was implemented throughout the industry, comic books became bland and limited in variation. As a result, the public was far less interested in the once exciting medium. Sales of comic books tumbled. Timely/Marvel, which had reluctantly joined the CMAA, was among those companies hard-hit by censorship. This turn of events led Goodman to abandon his newsstand distributor and form his own distribution operation, Atlas News Company.

Dealing with the many new changes in the comic-book field, Stan Lee continued to be a loyal, efficient employee. But the public outcry against comics made Stan even more aware that he was part of an industry that few people respected. Nevertheless, Stan kept his nose to the grindstone and pushed out the type of mild product that Goodman ordered. By the late 1940s and early 1950s, superhero comics had gone out of fashion, and Stan was creating comics in genres such as romance, women's stories, and Westerns (one of his favorites).

During this period—lasting until the early 1960s—Stan supervised, directed, and participated in the fast-paced, never-ending production line that kept Martin Goodman's comic-book division in business. The firm's offices in the Empire State Building had a room (the bull pen) where staff artists and writers worked at a furious pace, keeping up with the monthly schedule of established and new publications. To ensure that he always had enough new material on hand, Stan would backlog comics that could be used at a moment's notice. When it finally came to Goodman's attention that his company had a huge inventory of unpublished material, he forced good-natured Stan to fire several of the full-time staff, keeping some on a freelance basis. This was part of Goodman's efforts to cut costs in tough economic times.

As the marketplace changed in the 1950s, Stan continued to examine their competitors closely, hoping to mirror their successes and avoid their mistakes. In this way, Marvel weathered the storm. However, it was a bleak period in which Stan felt he was nothing more than a lead man involved in an uncreative operation.

What made this tough time bearable for Stan was his good working relationships with the artists and writers on his staff. In this stressful era, Stan developed a great friendship with the highly talented and versatile Joe Maneely, a top artist at Marvel who provided memorable art work for such magazine entries as *The Black Knight*. Sadly, the 32-year-old Maneely died in a grisly accident in 1958. Looking back on the loss of this gifted colleague and good friend, Stan admits, "I think if he hadn't died, I would have eventually maybe quit Marvel and gone off with Joe and done other [business] stuff."

In late 1956 Goodman signed a contract with a large comic-distribution firm, American News. A very short time later, American News went bankrupt. By then Goodman had irritated many other distributors who turned their backs on Martin's need to find a new middle-man to bring his comic books to newsstands. In a moment of panic, Goodman signed a bad deal with rival DC Comics and their own distribution firm, Independent News. Knowing that Goodman was desperate to keep his comic-book enterprise alive, DC demanded terms that were highly unfavorable to Goodman's operation. For example, the overwhelmed publisher agreed to cut back his comic-book product line to only eight titles published in any given month. This left the comic-book branch of Good-man's firm greatly reduced. As a result, operations had to be cut back further. Reluctantly, Stan had to fire more of his coworkers. In another money-saving step, the remaining comic-book division of Goodman's business moved to small offices on Madison Avenue.

During this troublesome period, Stan found a creative outlet for his frustration by writing scripts for the firm's latest comic-book trend, light-hearted science fiction tales such as *Tales to Astonish, Strange Tales,* and *Worlds of Fantasy.* Some of these releases were scripted by Stan's brother, Larry, who was freelancing for the company.

A Pleasant Diversion

During the 1950s workaholic Stan amused himself—and earned extra money—by writing light-hearted pieces for magazines. These offerings were typically nothing more than photographs with racy captions. He also moonlighted by writing scripts for giveaway promotional comic books for another publisher. Then, in 1961, under his own Madison Publications imprint, Stan turned out *Golfers Anonymous* and *Blushing Blurbs,* two slapped-together entries featuring stock photos with funny captions. These books (priced at $1.00 to $1.50 each) sold out their initial print runs. Yet for some reason (which Lee later attributed to his own lack of good business skills), he never went back for additional printings, which could have earned him a lot more profit with no extra work involved. Other similar Stan Lee publications were several issues of a magazine called *Monsters to Laugh With* and a series of paperbacks entitled *You Don't Say!* During this time, Stan also teamed with Dan DeCarlo briefly for a syndicated comic strip called "Willie Lumpkin." He also originated a syndicated strip called "Mrs. Lyon's Cubs," dealing with a pack of cub scouts.

As the 1960s began, Stan continued being a jack-of-all-trades for his demanding boss, Martin Goodman. By now, Stan was increasingly discouraged about his future, but he never experienced that dreaded fear of all authors: writer's block. According to Stan, "Whenever I have to write something, the words always seem to come to me. They may not be the right words, they may not even be good words . . . but I can't remember ever sitting and staring off into space trying in vain to think of something to write. There are so many words and thoughts available to us, it's never seemed all that difficult to grab some of them and put them to work."

As he approached age 40, Stan thought seriously of finally changing professions. In the midst of this midlife crisis, Martin Goodman walked into Stan's office. He mentioned that he had recently been on the golf course with Jack Liebowitz, head of DC Comics, and had learned that the rival company had done well with their new twist to a comic-book genre. The company had taken its trio of major superheroes—Batman, Superman, and Wonder Woman—and combined them with four other established characters into the Justice League of America, who, as a powerful team, fought the forces of evil. This superhero squad had been warmly received by comic-book buyers. Inspired by this success, Goodman suggested to Lee that their comic-book operation should also launch a combined group of superheroes.

A New Beginning

Stan was not very enthusiastic about this latest instruction from Martin Goodman. Suffering from burnout, Stan was in no mood to churn out more ripoffs of the competition. He was convinced it was time he moved on to other creative challenges. He discussed his career decision with his wife. Joan suggested that Goodman's demand might actually be a golden opportunity for Stan. She reasoned that her husband had nothing to lose by turning out a new comic-book entry in the format that he thought was appropriate and innovative, never mind what conservative, copycat Goodman wanted. As Joan reasoned, Stan had everything to gain if the new venture succeeded. The worst thing that could happen if it flopped was that Stan would be fired. And, she concluded, wasn't he already planning to quit the business anyway?

With his wife's encouragement, Stan jumped into action. He conferred with artist Jack Kirby (now back at Marvel), and *The Fantastic Four #1* (November 1961) was soon born. The new book focused on a quartet of fresh, distinctive characters all strangely affected when they are exposed to intense cosmic rays during a spaceflight: arrogant Reed Richards (Mr. Fantastic), his flighty wife Sue (Invisible Girl), Sue's hot-tempered brother Johnny (Human Torch), and Ben Grimm (The Thing), a rugged but kind-hearted man who transforms into a grotesque orange-colored being with tremendous strength. What made these superheroes so unique was that they each had very human flaws with which readers could quickly identify. As these characters coped with their various shortcomings (insensitivity, oafishness, scatterbrained attitudes, and self-consciousness), they had to tear themselves away from their own concerns to become heroes who combated the world's evil forces.

The Fantastic Four quickly grabbed readers' attention. As newsstand sales were tabulated, Goodman had to admit that he had been wrong in fighting Stan's efforts to break away from the traditional superheroes as flawless models of virtues. Goodman urged Stan to immediately create more of these humanized characters.

Freed from suffocating conventions, Stan let his imagination run wild. He and his crew of top-flight artists produced a series of new heroes: Mighty Thor; Ant Man; The Incredible Hulk; Dr. Strange; Silver Surfer, Iron Man (inspired by billionaire entrepreneur Howard Hughes); Sgt. Fury and His Howling Commandoes (which had a multi-ethnic cast of characters), Daredevil (a blind superhero); The Avengers; and a teaming of intriguing, constantly altering mutants known as the X-Men. In later years, Lee would acknowledge that it was no coincidence that so many of the superheroes' alter egos (for example, Peter Parker, Bruce Banner, and Reed Richards) had first and last names that started with the same letter. He explained that because of his notorious bad memory, it was often difficult for him to call to mind the full name of any of his many creations. But if he seized upon one name of the character, he knew that the other name started with the same letter and it gave him a helpful hint.

Beloved Spidey

Perhaps of all Stan's creative output in this fertile period, none was more satisfying and successful than the Amazing Spider-Man. The character made its first appearance in *Amazing Fantasy #15* (August 1962) with script by editor Stan Lee and art by Steve Ditko. As with Marvel Comics' other new superheroes, this character was full of failings that made him doubt his role as superhero.

Stan first experienced superhero success with the creation of
The Fantastic Four. (Photofest)

Moreover, Spider-Man's alter ego, Peter Parker, was a different type of teenager from the usual for comic books of the period. Usually when adolescents were involved with superheroes, they were categorized as sidekicks (such as Robin and Batman). They were rarely the center of the action or story. Peter Parker, however, is the main character in Spider-Man comics. Parker is a bright but nerdy high school youth who has been bitten by a radioactive spider. Although he now possesses superhuman powers, Parker still has a wide array of problems: keeping a girlfriend, dealing with his well-meaning but needy Aunt May, maintaining his studies and/or job while being distracted with fighting sinister forces, keeping his identity as Spider-Man a secret, and so forth.

One of the unique aspects of the Spider-Man comics was the emphasis placed on what Parker/Spider-Man was thinking about as he scaled the walls of a skyscraper, swung perilously between buildings on one of his webs, or stuck to a high ceiling while awaiting his adversaries. Through dialogue balloons filled with Parker's/Spidey's thoughts, readers gained tremendous insight into the troubled superhero. This gimmick, in particular, really made the web slinger spring to life. (What also lent realism to the Spider-Man adventures—and that of the other Marvel characters dreamed up by Stan Lee and his team of artists—was that the action took place in or around Manhattan rather than in some fictional city such as Gotham or Metropolis.)

For Stan, Spider-Man was, and would remain, his greatest contribution to comic-book history. Ironically, Martin Goodman had initially opposed Stan's new comic-book character, claiming the public hated spiders and did not want an adolescent hero as the central figure—especially not one who had so many personal problems. But as Stan says of Spidey, "One reason he's so successful is that absolutely sensational costume created by Steve Ditko. It's a perfect costume. Spider-Man is probably the only superhero whose body is totally covered by a costume.

The character of Spider-Man (seen here in the 2004 film Spider-Man 2) remains Stan's most significant contribution to comic-book history. (Photofest)

You don't see any flesh at all. Therefore, he could be Asian; he could be black; he could be an American Indian; he could have any color skin. So anybody reading the story could imagine, 'This could be me.' That wasn't planned but that may well have something to do with his popularity all around the world."

On another occasion, a proud Stan told an interviewer, "I'm not comparing myself to Walt Disney, but whenever anybody thinks of Disney, the first thing that comes to mind is Mickey Mouse. Whenever people introduce me to somebody, they say, 'This is the guy who did Spider-Man'—even though I've done a hundred million other things. But I'm very flattered."

6

KING OF THE UNIVERSE

With the huge success of Stan Lee's collaborative achievements in the world of comic-book superheroes, Marvel Comics was once again turning out product that put it at the forefront of the industry. For example, in 1961 Marvel sold 7 million copies of its books; the next year their circulation increased to 13 million. In a moment of self-congratulations, Stan and Goodman added a slogan to the cover of *The Fantastic Four*, stating it was "The World's Greatest Comic." The motto caught on and soon was applied to every Marvel product.

As the 1960s progressed, Marvel was front and center as *the* comic-book publisher, proclaiming that it had created the "Marvel Age of Comics" in which there was a Marvel Universe of superheroes. Readers were excited by Marvel's new books and wrote enthusiastic fan letters. A natural salesman, Stan seized on this positive public response to foster a connection between comic-book buyers and management at the publishers. He promoted the letters-to-the-editor section (and the "Bullpen Bulletins" and "Stan's Soapbox" pages) of each magazine and personalized it in a humorous, friendly, and entertaining style. It was at this time that he came up with the notion of signing his editorials and other communications with "excelsior," an Old English word meaning "Upward and Onward to Greater Glory!" Because Stan used it so often and it caught on so well with fans, the expression came to be closely associated with him.

Stan also started an official fan club for enthusiasts of Marvel Comics. The Merry Marvel Marching Society (MMMS) operated successfully for several years until new corporate management decided it could be dispensed with—against Stan's wishes. Also in this era, when readers wrote in pointing out a flub in the logic of the plot or character development in a Marvel book, Stan began sending these letter writers special replies: an empty envelope which was stamped "Congratulations! This envelope contains a genuine Marvel Comics No-Prize, which you have just won!"

The Marvel Method

In light of Marvel Comics bounce back into prosperity, Stan couldn't perform all of the tasks he once had, especially since he was almost a one-man executive/creative staff leader. To ease things a bit, Stan refined a system he had been developing to keep his in-house and freelance staffs constantly busy and not stuck waiting for an opportunity to confer with him. He called this the Marvel Method.

In this system, Stan, as the writer, would discuss the basic plot for an upcoming comic book entry with the artist. The latter then went off and drew the entire story with no script at hand. When Stan received the art, he would then write the text that filled the characters' dialogue balloons and the captions. Often, the artist would have taken the characters and plot in a different direction than Stan had imagined. It usually worked well, however, as the method gave the artist the freedom to utilize all his own creativity and input.

As Stan grew even busier, he turned over some of the script writing to others who, in turn, employed the Marvel Method. In fact, Stan's smart idea was adopted by many other companies in the industry.

Despite the reality that Marvel was a production-line operation, the rejuvenated, enthusiastic Stan repeatedly reminded his staff that "When working with a colorful cast of comicbook characters, they mustn't be depicted in a clichéd way." According to Stan, "Most of the fun was coming up with surprising twists and turns. In fact, one of

Using Stan's Marvel Method, Marvel became the leading comic-book publisher in the early 1960s, producing some of the most famous titles in comic-book history. (Photofest)

the best rules of thumb was, create the kind of characters that would work well in a dramatic television series." (This practical advice would prove valuable in the coming years, when several of the Marvel Universe of Super-heroes became the basis of TV shows and feature films.)

Because of the huge popularity of the Marvel Comics superheroes, Stan felt able to develop another innovation—he extended particularly exciting episodes beyond the confines of one comic-book issue into two or three monthly installments. The cliffhanging gimmick worked well with the public and became another industry standard.

In the book *Stan Lee and the Rise and Fall of the American Comic Book*, co-authors Jordan Raphael and Tom Spurgeon point out that Stan's writing during this period was also innovative. They point out that Stan's writing engaged readers, ". . . praising them for their intimate knowledge of past adventures and the high standards they brought to the work in front of them. . . ." Once again, Stan Lee had taken comic books in new and respected directions.

Changes on the Horizons

In life nothing stays the same for an indefinite period. It was no different at Marvel Comics. In the mid-1960s Marvel Comics moved to a new space on Madison Avenue. Stan remained Marvel's editor in chief, art director, and script writer for many of the firm's titles. However, some members of his staff were growing restless. One of these was the highly regarded artist Steve Ditko, who had done the original Spider-Man art work. Ditko was unhappy that he was not receiving more credit or more income at Marvel. He grumbled that in interviews, Stan (who had become the company's spokesperson) received the bulk of attention. Ditko felt that all anyone remembered was the name Stan Lee. In 1966 Ditko left Marvel. It started a running controversy between Stan and Steve and their respective groups of followers, creating waves of bad feeling between the two camps that has never been fully resolved.

A similar dispute occurred between Lee and Jack Kirby, especially after this veteran artist left Marvel for a final time in 1978. Over the years, the quarrel escalated with each camp (including whoever was the latest corporate owner of Marvel) eager to push its own point of view. The debate raged over the artist's overall impact in the creation of a comic-book character and how this affected the valuable copyright ownership. When Kirby died in February 1994, the ongoing disagreement was still burning. To this day, the role of the artist in comic books causes heated discussion among comic-book fans, pop culture historians, and industry attorneys. For a time the fallout from these disputes sullied the reputation of Stan Lee as the creator of a host of marvelous comic-book characters.

While these 1960s industry changes were occurring, Stan was busy becoming "Mr. Marvel Comics" to the world at large. Not only had his standing in the business jumped higher, thanks to his many interviews on behalf of Marvel and their products, but he was winning several honors at the Alley Awards, a fan-based awards event. At the same time, Stan had begun a career as a successful lecturer. This was a result of the MMMS fan clubs and their chapters at many U.S. colleges. These MMMS suggested that Stan be contracted to highlight campus lectures. Always happy to meet the public and spend time recounting the history of Marvel Comics, Stan began accepting lecture dates. Before long he was doing a lecture almost every week somewhere in the United States and was being paid up to $3,000 per speaking engagement. Eventually Stan had to hire a lecture bureau agent to book these personal appearances. This all added to the growing fame of "Stan the Man," who was becoming the face of the comic-book industry.

On a personal level, Stan was experiencing his own changes. In the mid-1960s, after 20 years of living on Long Island, Stan and Joan wanted to be back in New York City so that their teenaged daughter could take full advantage of all that Manhattan had to offer. They purchased a condo in the city and, later, purchased a small house in the Hamptons on Long Island for weekend retreats. At about this time, Stan's father, Jack, who had never remarried after his wife's death, passed away.

Marvel's New Bosses

In the autumn of 1968, Martin Goodman sold Marvel to the Perfect Film and Chemical Corporation. As part of the deal, Goodman stayed on as president/publisher of Magazine Management (the publishing division of the holding company) but not of Marvel Comics. Part of Goodman's deal required that Stan Lee sign an agreement that he would remain with Marvel. In retrospect, Stan wishes he had listened to advisers who told him he could have made sizeable financial and management demands that would have secured his financial and career future. However, happy-go-lucky, impatient, trusting Stan thought he could count on Goodman to do right by him in the years to come. Thus, Stan signed a three-year pact with the new management but did not press points regarding his own wants.

Thinking about this period, Stan wonders why he never heeded the sound advice of Marshall Finck, a good friend and highly successful business executive. Finck repeatedly told Stan that he should quit Marvel and "form your own company," using his reputation and experience to find backing for such an enterprise. Stan's response to the suggestion was that "such an idea would have been alien to me. . . . To me, just having a good, steady job, feeling that I was wanted, needed by some company, was the ultimate mark of success, of security."

In the coming years, Perfect Film would change its name to Cadence Industries, and a new executive would be placed in charge. But unlike the past one, or Martin

Goodman before him, he lacked a strong vision for Marvel Comics. Still, Stan was offered and accepted the position of publisher at Marvel Comics, a post Martin Goodman had hoped would go to his youngest son, Chip.

One of Stan's first acts as publisher was to remove himself from many of the day-to-day chores of running Marvel's creative side. He appointed the young Roy Thomas as the firm's new editor in chief, one of several to hold that post in coming years. For the next 15 years Stan focused on promoting the name of Marvel Comics, making deals with merchandizing firms, negotiating movie and TV adaptations of Marvel properties, and promoting the brand name of Marvel Comics to the world.

Stan's new work priorities took him across the United States and Canada, as well as frequent treks to Europe. He maintained his growing schedule of lecture engagements and even hosted an evening at Carnegie Hall. On that occasion, a promoter convinced Stan to be the focal figure at an event called a

One of many young fans enjoys a comic book. (Corbis)

"Marvel-ous Evening with Stan Lee" on January 5, 1972. Unfortunately, the event included a string of guest musical artists who had nothing to do with the world of comic books. The poorly structured evening failed to meet anyone's expectations. On the other hand, a few years later, Stan realized his celebrity status when he arrived in Mexico City for one of his colorful speaking engagements. There he was provided with six bodyguards to keep him from being mobbed by the crowds.

Although Stan was no longer devoting much time to scripting or supervising the monthly installments of Marvel Comics, he did keep in touch with this creative aspect of the business. In early 1977 he began a syndicated daily comic strip of the Spider-Man character with John Romita as his artist collaborator. The next year Stan reteamed with Jack Kirby to produce a novel-length version of the Silver Surfer character.

Stan Lee, Author

By the 1970s Stan had authored several books. In 1974 came *Origin of Marvel Comics*. Its success led to the sequels *Son of the Origin of Marvel Comics* (1975) and *Grandson of the Origin of Marvel Comics* (1998), as well as such additional Marvel histories as *Bring on the Bad Guys* (1976) and *The Superhero Women* (1977). In 1978 Lee teamed with artist John Buscema for the book *How to*

Draw Comics the Marvel Way, which set forth principles for people wanting to draw comic-strip/-book characters. In this illustrated guide, Stan cautioned, "Just being able to draw the figure is only half the job. When you're drawing comicbook superhero sagas, you've got to be able to move it—to animate it—to put it in action!" He also included such practical advice as, "Because of the importance of the [comic-book] cover, and because it serves as a full-color advertisement for the magazine itself, all the elements of the illustration must be very carefully put together."

While these books satisfied Lee's urge to be Marvel's historian and comic-book-artist instructor, he was most proud of his efforts to bring about social awareness in the early 1970s. In three consecutive issues of *The Amazing Spider-Man* in 1971, Stan had Peter Parker dealing with the drug addiction of his college roommate and friend, Harry Osborn. In publishing these installments, Marvel went against the rules of the still very conservative Comics Code Authority (a branch of the CMAA). Before releasing these issues, Stan met the censorship group and informed them that representatives of the U.S. Department of Health, Education and Welfare had urged him and Marvel to tackle the anti-drug theme. Despite the government's request, the CCA refused to give these Marvel issues their stamp of approval. Defying the organization, Marvel published them without the industry sanction, which helped to bring around a great reduction in the power and influence of the CCA.

When dealing with a controversial social issue like drugs proved effective with readers, Marvel added other Spider-Man adventures involving prison riots and racial discrimination. Such hot topics also proved to be a fresh avenue for Marvel Comics to attract new readers in the constantly changing comic-book marketplace of the 1970s. The company also produced comic-book entries that featured superheroes who were African American (Luke Cage, Hero for Hire), Native American (Red Wolf), and female (Shanna the She Devil). The firm also took advantage of fresh pop culture trends, such as an interest in kung-fu, to produce new genre books (*Iron Fist*).

As the 1970s progressed, Stan continued to remove himself from most day-to-day activity at Marvel, especially the financial aspects for which he felt he had little aptitude. He contented himself with being chief adviser to his ever-growing staff of artists and writers, many of them young talent who had grown up reading, appreciating, and studying the work of Stan and his artist collaborators.

By now Stan Lee had parlayed a temporary job into a highly successful, four-decade career, and it was far from over.

7

SPRINGING INTO THE NEW MILLENNIUM

Comic-book publishers already knew that comics provided material for valuable feature films, serials, cartoon, and radio series. In the mid-1960s, Marvel Comics was aggressive in bringing several of its superhero characters into the country's most popular medium: television.

Superheroes of the Small Screen

The year 1966 saw the debut of the TV series *The Marvel Superheroes*. This cheaply made animated series presented five of the company's most popular characters: Captain America, The Incredible Hulk, Iron Man, The Mighty Thor, and Sub-Mariner. Each was featured in 13 half-hour episodes, creating a total of 65 entries. Much more memorable was the Hulk's reemergence in 1978 in a live-action TV show, *The Incredible Hulk*. The CBS series ran for four seasons and inspired three made-for-TV features with the same leads. It also led to a 1982–85 Saturday morning NBC-TV animated series and was often paired with another new half-hour animated entry licensed from Marvel—*The Amazing Spider-Man*. Later, from 1996 to 1999 on the UPN TV network, there was a new animated version of *The Incredible Hulk*.

Meanwhile, in 1967, Marvel's famed quartet, The Fantastic Four, made their TV debut as a half-hour animated series on ABC-TV, followed a decade later by a new cartoon version on NBC. In the fall of 1977 Marvel's Spider-Man returned to the limelight in the form of a TV movie/series pilot, starring Nicholas Hammond as hero Peter Parker, now a college student. This led to a brief TV series (*The Amazing Spider-Man*) that ran occasionally in 1978 and 1979 but met with little interest.

Thanks to the whopping success of the live-action *Superman: The Movie* (1978) there was renewed interest in all comic-book superheroes. This prompted two live-action Captain America movies on CBS-TV in 1979, both pilots for a projected television series.

In all the preceding TV productions, Marvel Comics had merely contracted other firms to make the actual screen adaptations. Marvel also negotiated options with many other film/TV production companies for ventures

Many of Stan's comic-book creations became the basis of television series and feature films. (Photofest)

that never materialized. Over the years it had usually been Stan Lee whom Marvel had dispatched to Hollywood to scout out such production deals. Now in his 50s and with his college lecture schedule winding down, Stan enjoyed working with film and television studios on potential productions. When one of these projects came to reality, Stan would be brought in, sometimes as a preproduction consultant and/or given a screen credit of one sort or another.

Show business stirred Stan's creative juices, as well as his desire to gain the prestige that toiling in the comic-book industry had denied him. Once again he dreamed of becoming a screenwriter or, perhaps, a film director or even a packager of projects based on any of the many Marvel characters.

While Stan and his wife Joan were in Los Angeles in May 1979 on one of his many business trips to the West Coast, their New York City condo was robbed. What made the break-in all the more upsetting was that the burglars had stolen a hefty amount of Joan's jewelry, none of which had been insured. This incident, and the fact that most of Stan's work now took place in Los Angeles, convinced the Lees to relocate to southern California as soon as possible.

By now Marvel Comics, like much of the comic-book industry, was suffering yet another decline in sales, and a good deal of its current profits came from the lucrative licensing of its properties to others. At this point, executives at Marvel decided to form the company's own facility for animated TV shows, which could also provide a home for other individuals' animated projects. In 1980 Marvel set up an animation studio in Los Angeles and Stan agreed willingly to be in charge of the operation.

The Lees first took up residence in a condo near Beverly Hills, then settled into a spacious hillside home above the Sunset Strip that boasted a swimming pool, a guest house, and a wonderful view of the city's skyline. Stan realized with satisfaction that he had come a long way from his tiny childhood apartment in the Bronx, with its dreary view of another building.

Hollywood Dealmaker

Once established in Los Angeles, Stan devoted much of his time to Marvel's animation division, which turned out *Spider-Man and His Amazing Friends* (1981–86), *G.I. Joe* (1983–86), and *Muppet Babies* (1984–91). Eventually, in the changeover of regimes at Marvel, the animation studio would be shut down in 1990.

Meanwhile, in the 1980s Stan pushed hard to show his abilities as a Hollywood big shot, able to engineer major negotiations on Marvel's behalf. However, as with his long-time desire to write novels or plays, being a shrewd, well-disciplined movie dealmaker did not seem to be Stan's strong suit. Many of his ideas remained just that. The four feature film deals he did get for Marvel were creative—and financial—disappointments: *Howard the Duck* (1986), *The Punisher* (1989), *Captain America* (1991), and *The Fantastic Four,* a project rushed into filming at the last minute for legal and financial reasons. (The movie was so bad that it was never officially released anywhere, although bootleg prints of the film cropped up later.) Meanwhile, Marvel's flagship character, Spider-Man, had embarked on a torturous path of being optioned by first one and then another film producer or studio, eventually ending up in a legal tangle that was not resolved until the late 1990s.

Stan signing photos for fans (Associated Press)

Stan grew very sensitive about his losing streak in the world of Hollywood, which also included his many failed script ideas, treatments, and screenplays that tried to take advantage of new cinema trends. In 2000, Stan told Kenneth Plume in an extended interview (published on the website http://www.filmforce.ign.com) that his bad track record in Hollywood was a result of the ever-changing corporate ownership and management of the once well-run Marvel Comics. According to Stan: "The people back in New York who made these decisions—these contracts—gave the rights to do the movies to the wrong people. I mean, they took a valuable character like Captain America and they allowed a company to do it as a low-budget, quickie movie. They took *The Punisher*—which could have been good—and again, it was a low-budget movie. It was just a thing that was batted out. The only time we had a bigger budget movie [*Howard the Duck*] we were just unfortunate."

More Changing Times

In many ways, the comic-book industry was a long way from what it had been in its prime era of the 1940s and 1950s. For example, while the business had annual sales of 600 million copies in the early 1950s, by the start of the 1980s that annual figure had dropped to 150 million. As so many alternate forms of home entertainment developed (for instance, VHS tapes and laser discs, video games, camcorders, and the gradual growth of the personal computer and the emerging technology of the Internet), the public's interest in comic books was greatly diminished. It also did not help the comic-book trade that the cost of its magazines was always rising. Thus comics were no longer an inexpensive form of entertainment, especially if a reader bought them regularly.

The locations where comic books were being sold had also changed. Once, the product had been featured on newsstand racks in most neighborhoods. However, with the advent of underground comics, especially in the 1970s, specialty shops opened that featured the new brands of comics and, later, carried the more standard product of Marvel, DC, and the other established names in the field. As time passed, the specialty comic-book shops around the nation (especially in bigger cities) became the main places to find any type of comic product.

While comic books were losing their place as a major pastime for the new generations of young readers, there was a steady increase of sales to comic-book collectors, who are generally older than the once typical comic-book buyers. These determined buyers hoarded multiple issues of items they felt would one day sell for large amounts. This led to a collector-purchasing frenzy. Thrilled to have found a new target audience to acquire their releases (and trading cards and other collectibles), the comic-book publishers—both underground and traditional—began catering increasingly to collectors.

This trend caused a major backlash in the mid-1990s, when the high prices of collectible comics (some of which had reached into thousands of dollars) burst. When large numbers of collectors started selling their prized first editions and special issues, they soon discovered that the marketplace was flooded. Suddenly, people who once bought multiple copies of any and all new comic-book publications found investment avenues elsewhere. In turn, the specialty comic-book shops discovered they had lost a good portion of their steady customers. By the late 1990s, the number of existing specialty shops had dropped significantly. Since fewer newsstands were stocking comic books and many comic-book shops closed, it was difficult for publishers to attract new readers.

As these depressing changes occurred within the industry, Marvel Comics suffered, as did its rivals Dark Horse, DC, and Image. To survive the latest economic fallout, Marvel had to further streamline its operations. A good deal of this change happened during the time of Marvel editor in chief Jim Shooter, during the 1970s and 1980s. Among the many problems he faced was dealing with the relationship between the publisher and comic-book artists and writers, who now demanded more control, profit participation, and visibility in their jobs.

Stan Lee—1990s Style

As the 1990s began, Marvel made all of its big decisions out of its East Coast offices. Stan, based 3,000 miles away in Los Angeles, felt increasingly out of the loop of new activities with his long-time employer. Management came and went, but each team found it useful to keep Stan on as the firm's well-paid and highly visible spokesperson. He could be counted on to recite to the media the history of both Marvel and the comic-book industry. Stan would speak at the industry forums called ComicCons, and he welcomed potential partners in film and TV, while other Marvel employees made the actual deals. Typically, Stan received a token screen credit for the project at hand to demonstrate that he endorsed the production.

Always the showman, Stan also got a kick out of his occasional acting assignments. He narrated Marvel-based TV programs (for instance, 1982's *The Incredible Hulk* animated TV series) and made cameo appearances in movies (for instance, 1990's *The Ambulance*, 1995's *Mallrats*, 2000's *The X-Men*, 2003's *The Hulk* and *Daredevil*, and 2004's *Spider-Man 2*).

Through all of this, Stan Lee's name, face, and reputation remained very much a part of the comic-book industry as

Stan (right) on the set on Spider-Man *(2002) with fellow executive producer Avi Arad* (Photofest)

it trudged through the 1990s. In this period, Marvel's name was associated increasingly with big-budgeted box-office product that created screen franchises and massive merchandise licensing deals. These included *Blade* (1998) and its 2002 and 2004 follow-ups; *X-Men* (2000) and *X2* (2003); *Spider-Man* (2002) and its sequel *Spider-Man 2* (2004); *The Hulk* (2003); *Daredevil* (2003); *The Punisher* (2004); and

Man-Thing (2004); and future movie projects *The Fantastic Four, Iron Man, Ghost Rider,* and *Spider-Man 3.*

Unable to break his habit of scripting comics, Stan wrote occasional issues of an ongoing comic book (*Ravage 2099*) and continued writing a syndicated newspaper comic-strip version of *Spider-Man* that began in 1977. He also found time to participate in assorted how-to and comic-book history CD-ROM and DVD projects dealing with the history of Marvel and his many contributions to the industry. In 2000, Stan contracted with DC Comics to undertake a series of alternate interpretations of established DC superheroes such as Superman, Wonder Woman, and Batman. The unique project, which teamed Lee with major artists in the field, was entitled *Just Imagine Stan Lee Creating . . . .*

After many false starts over the decades, Stan finally channeled his energies into writing (with George Mair) his autobiography. When *Excelsior! The Amazing Life of Stan Lee* was published in 2002, *Library Journal* judged, "Throughout, the persona Lee created never falters; the tone is warm, straight-talking, and simultaneously confident and insecure, the same traits with which Lee imbued his superheroes." The review also noted that the memoir allowed its subject to address charges that he had grabbed too much credit for the creation of the Marvel superheroes.

Dot-com Disaster

In 1999, after decades of being a Marvel employee and now having the figurehead title of chairman emeritus, Stan Lee was in his late seventies. Marvel (then undergoing bankruptcy proceedings) paid him up to $1 million yearly to be a company spokesman. He received an additional $125,000 yearly from Marvel for writing the ongoing "Spider-Man" comic strip. Not content with his lack of day-to-day power within the industry he had so long promoted, Stan eagerly jumped into a business venture that proved to be a very bad choice.

In January 1999 Stan formed Stan Lee Media Inc., based in Los Angeles. The startup company was designed to use the powers of the Internet to create online fan clubs, Web-based animated strips, drawings, and games featuring new Lee-devised superheroes, among other things. One of Stan's partners in this undertaking was Peter Paul, a man—unknown to Stan—who had a clouded past. The new operation generated a lot of excitement as big plans were made for online animated properties such as *The 7th Portal* (about a team of superheroes and villains), *Police Force 2220* (focusing on a futuristic vision of crime fighting), *The Accuser* (revolving around a wheelchair-bound attorney with a special protective suit), and *Stan's Evil Clone*.

Stan Lee Media Inc. soon became a hotly traded item on the U.S. stock market, jumping up to $31 a share and making Lee a very wealthy (about $90 million) man on paper. Then in November 2000 the bubble suddenly burst. The company had spent a lot more than it earned. As with many other startup Internet-based businesses of the time, Stan Lee Media Inc. crashed disastrously. Before the NASDAQ stock exchange halted trading of the company's shares in mid-December, the company's stock price had fallen to 13 cents per share. By January 2001 the Securities and Exchange Commission was investigating Stan Lee Media, in particular Peter Paul (special consultant) and Stephen Gordon (ex-executive vice president of operations). Gordon and other alleged criminal associates were later arrested on charges of fraud and stock manipulation. By then Paul had fled to Brazil, where he was later arrested and subject to trial in the United States. Throughout the whole nightmare, it was never proved that Stan had participated in—let alone been aware of—any of the wrongdoings associated with Stan Lee Media Inc., and he was never charged with any offense. Nevertheless, it was a horrendous experience. A very embarrassed Stan would say, in retrospect, "That was the biggest disappointment of my life" and "I'll never be so stupidly trusting again!"

Facing the Future

The pain of the Stan Lee Media Inc. disaster was partially erased for Stan by the box-office success of *Spider-Man* in spring 2002 and the news that *Spider-Man 2* (2004) was already in the works. When released, *Spider-Man 2* generated terrific reviews. The new production made even more money than its predecessor. The success of the big-screen *Spider-Man* films launched a rash of new deals to put Marvel superheroes on the big and little screens, with a vast array of merchandise tie-ins and even plans to produce *Spider-Man* as a Broadway musical. Suddenly Stan was big news again in Hollywood. Once more he was much in demand for interviews, a situation that continued as other Marvel characters, such as The Incredible Hulk and Daredevil, were adapted into major motion pictures. Once more feeling on top of the world, Stan instituted a hefty lawsuit against Marvel in November 2002. He claimed that by the terms of his 1998 employment pact with Marvel, he was entitled to 10 percent of the company's profits from the use of its characters in both movies and TV shows, but that Marvel allegedly had not lived up to the terms of the deal. (In January 2005, a U.S. District court ruled that Marvel had unjustly deprived Lee of profits that Spider-Man and other characters had generated over the past seven years. Stan was happy with the decision, which could generate millions of dollars for him. Meanwhile, Marvel announced plans to appeal the verdict.)

While that complex case was working its way through the legal system, a still-energetic Stan developed a new

cable-based animated TV series that featured the voice of
Pamela Anderson. This cartoon show was one of many
projects that the 80-year-old Stan had devised for his new
production company, POW! Entertainment. (POW! stood
for Purveyors of Wonder!) Stan's ambitious plans for POW!
also anticipated a series of other broadcast and direct-to-
DVD properties to be produced under the title of *Stan Lee
Presents.*

*Stan Lee is considered by many to be the father of modern
comic books.* (Wire Image)

Still extremely young-at-heart and buoyant, Stan Lee, considered by many to be the father of modern comic books, points out, "People ask, why not retire? Most people retire because now at last they'll be able to do what they want to do. But I am doing what I want to do." He also notes, "I'm working on so many new things. The one thing I love to do is come up with ideas for characters and for stories. . . . Now I have the chance to be creating more things, and it's a tremendous amount of fun."

TIME LINE*

1922   Born Stanley Martin Lieber in Manhattan, on December 28, the first of two children

1939   Graduates from DeWitt Clinton High School in the Bronx; begins working as an office boy for a clothing manufacturer in Manhattan's garment district

1940   Hired as office gofer by Timely Publications, the comic-book division of publishing enterprises owned by Martin Goodman (Stanley's relative)

1941   First short story published in *Captain America Comics*—uses pseudonym Stan Lee, which becomes his official name at work and in private life; contributes script to "Headline Hunter, Foreign Correspondent" for *Captain America Comics #5*; appointed "temporary" editor/art director/scripter of firm's comic-book publications

1942 In November enlists in the U.S. Army and is assigned to the Signal Corps to write training manuals/films; initially based in Astoria, New York; later assigned to a North Carolina military post and then to one in Indiana

1943 In free time throughout military service, moonlights for Timely by scripting comic books

1945 Receives an honorable discharge from the army in September; returns to working for Timely as editor in chief/art director/scripter of comic books; rents own Manhattan living quarters

1947 In December weds British-born Joan Clayton Boocock, a hat model. Article: "There's Money in Comics"; Book: *The Secrets Behind the Comics*

1948 Moves to Hewlett Harbor, Long Island, with Joan and his younger brother, Larry, following mother's death

1949 As superhero comic books lose popularity after World War II, follows the lead of rival publishers in turning out comic-book publications focusing on romance, women's stories, crime, and Western genres

1950 Works part of the week for Timely from Long Island home; daughter Joan Celia is born

1953   In reaction to increased activities by government and public anti-comic-book groups, writes attacks on censorship organizations within pages of Timely Comics; second daughter, Jan, dies three days after birth

1956   Atlas (the new name for Martin Goodman's Timely operation) abandons its in-house distribution setup; firm forced to sign a highly restrictive contract with the distribution arm of rival DC Comics; many cutbacks at Goodman's comic-book division, pushing more work on Stan, who finds diversion in scripting science-fiction comic-book entries (e.g., _Tales to Astonish_ and _Worlds of Fantasy_)

1961   Collaborates with artist Jack Kirby on _The Fantastic Four #1_ comic book released late in year; freelances beyond comic-book editorial/writing duties. Books: _Blushing Blurbs_ and _Golfers Anonymous_. Syndicated newspaper comic strips: "Mrs. Lyon's Cubs" and "Willie Lumpkin"

1962   The success of the Fantastic Four leads to teaming with artist Steve Ditko for the Spider-Man comic-book property. Books: _You Don't Say!_ series

1963   With various artists as teammates, continues throughout the 1960s to produce new properties for Martin Goodman's Marvel Comics; the Marvel

Universe of Superheroes soon includes, among others: The Ant Man; The Avengers; Black Panther; Daredevil; The Incredible Hulk; Mighty Thor; Quicksilver; and The X-Men. Book: *More You Don't Say!*

1964   Magazines: *Monsters to Laugh With* series, later revived in 1970s as *Monster Madness*

1966   As the spokesperson for Marvel Comics promotes a fan club (Merry Marvel Marching Society), in house refines the use of "the Marvel Method" to give artists more creative freedom and escalate production. TV series: animated *The Marvel Superheroes* (ABC), the first of several television shows based on Marvel Comics' superheroes

1968   Marvel Comics sold to Perfect Film and Chemical Corporation (aka Cadence Industries) with Stan still editor in chief/art director/scripter; moves with family to Manhattan summer home in the Hamptons

1971   *The Amazing Spider-Man* comic books tackle the controversial subject of drug abuse and are published without the sanction of the Comics Code Authority (CCA); a founding member of Academy of Comic Book Arts; writes screenplays with Alain Resnais and Lloyd Kaufman, none of which are produced

1972   As publisher of Marvel Comics—and later briefly its president—delegates many of company's day-to-day chores; expands activities as Marvel's spokesperson, including lecturing on Marvel Comics on the college campus circuit

1973   Wins awards from Academy of Comic Books Arts. Feature Film: *Year 01*—narrator

1974   Book: *Origin of Marvel Comics*

1975   Book: *Son of the Origin of Marvel Comics*

1976   Book: *Bring on the Bad Guys*

1977   Fosters TV movie *Spider-Man* (ABC) which leads to *The Amazing Spider-Man* (ABC) teleseries the next year. Book: *The Superhero Women*. Syndicated newspaper comic-strip: "Spider-Man"

1978   Live-action TV series *The Incredible Hulk* (CBS) series begins a four-year TV run. Book: (Co-authors with artist John Buscema) *How to Draw Comics the Marvel Way*

1979   Another Marvel Comics' property, Captain America, is the basis of two made-for-TV movies (CBS)

1980   Marvel Comics establishes its own animation studio in Hollywood with Stan in charge; the Lees relocate to Los Angeles

1981 TV: *Spider-Man and His Amazing Friends* (NBC)—narrator of animated series from 1981 to 1986

1982 TV: *The Incredible Hulk* (NBC)—narrator of animated series from 1982 to 1985

1986 Helps to launch feature film *Howard the Duck* (Universal)

1989 A negotiator in deals that leads to theatrical features *The Punisher* (New World) and *Captain America* (released theatrically abroad in 1991 but only on home entertainment formats in the United States; TV: *The Trial of the Incredible Hulk* (CBS)—cameo

1990 Feature film: *The Ambulance* (MGM/UA)—cameo

1994 Involved with setting up feature film *The Fantastic Four* (New Horizon) which is never released officially. Feature film: *Jugular Wine* (Pagan)—cameo

1995 Feature film: *Mallrats* (Gramercy)—cameo

1997 TV series: animated *The Incredible Hulk* (UPN)—cameo

1998 Signs a new non-exclusive pact with Marvel Comics to remain as company's chairman emeritus and spokesperson. Book: (with others) *Grandson of the Origin of Marvel Comics*. TV series: animated *Spider-Man* (Fox)—cameo

1999 Co-founder of Stan Lee Media Inc., a startup Internet-based operation

2000 By year's end, Stan Lee Media Inc. stops trading on the U.S. Stock exchange. Feature films: *The Adventures of Cinderella's Daughter* (Creative Light)—cameo, *Citizen Toxie: The Toxic Avenger IV* (Troma)—narrator; *X-Men* (20th Century- Fox)—cameo. Online Web Series: animated *The 7th Portal*—cameo. Video game: *Spider-Man*—voice

2001 Video game: *Spider-Man II: Enter Electro*—voice

2002 Helps to promote theatrical film *Spider-Man* (Columbia); files lawsuit against Marvel Enterprises for alleged violations of the terms of the 1998 pact with Lee. Book: (with George Mair) *Excelsior! The Amazing Life of Stan Lee*

2003 Scripts new animated TV series, *Stripperella* (Spike TV), a product of new business enterprise, POW! Entertainment. Feature Films: *Daredevil* (20th Century-Fox)—cameo and *The Hulk* (Universal)—cameo; TV series: *Mad TV* (Fox)—guest appearance, animated *Spider-Man* (MTV)

2004 Participates in promotional efforts for *The Punisher* (Lions Gate) and *Spider-Man 2* (Columbia)—also cameo; listed in the credits of several feature films based on Marvel Comics superheroes that he helped to co-create, including: *The Fantastic Four, Iron Man, Man-Thing, The Hands of Shang-Chi, Ghost Rider,* and *Spider-Man 3.* Feature film: *The Princess Diaries 2: Royal Engagement* (Buena Vista)—cameo

2005 Wins lawsuit against Marvel Enterprises in U.S. Federal Court; *Elektra* (20th Century-Fox), a big-screen spinoff from the *Daredevil* property, is released, with Lee credited as executive producer

* Many of the Marvel Comics superheroes comic books on which Stan Lee collaborated were later reprinted in various book editions. Of many of the feature films, TV series, and made-for TV movies based on Marvel Comics superheroes, Lee received various credited and/or uncredited billing as writer of original character(s), executive producer, or con-sultant.

HOW TO BECOME A COMIC-BOOK WRITER

THE JOB

Like all those who work with the written word, comic-book writers are first and foremost good communicators. Specifically, comic-book writers are creative storytellers who possess both a strong command of language and a good visual sense. Although comic-book writers do not have to be (and often are not) good visual artists, they must be able to weave engaging stories that can be rendered in lively artwork and told within a limited number of comic-book panels. These challenges are unique to comic-book writers, but it is a love of these challenges and the comic-book form that attracts writers to this field.

Comic-book writing, like all creative processes, starts with an idea. Writers may have an idea for an entirely new comic book, or they may think of stories and plots for an existing comic-book series or character. Developing strong characters is one of the essential steps in creating a good comic-book story, especially if the characters will be part of a comic-book series. Before writing a specific plot, a comic-book writer develops an in-depth profile and back-story for the main character. For example, one of the most popular types of comic-book characters is the superhero. Among other things, the writer must decide on the hero's background, general physical appearance (both as a superhero and as an everyday citizen, if the character has such a dual nature), powers (and how they came to be), weaknesses or flaws, enemies, love interests, costume, day job, means of transport, and so forth. In addition, the writer will invent a cast of recurring minor characters, such as a wise-cracking boss, nosy neighbor, or faithful sidekick. The writer must also carefully plan the setting of the comic book (urban metropolis, another planet, medieval times, and so forth). A writer's careful consideration of even the smallest details will make a comic book much more engaging and believable for readers—even if it is primarily a fantastic tale. Working out these details will also make it easier for a writer to communicate his or her ideas to the comic-book artists (called pencillers and inkers) who will actually draw the story.

After writers have developed the main character and the "world" of the comic book, they can begin to focus on stories and plots. Sometimes writers come up with these ideas through genuine inspiration, but stories for established comic-book series are often the result of a brainstorming session between writers and comic-book editors. (Among other things, editors come up with story ideas; evaluate ideas from freelance writers and artists; review the art and language used in comic books; and ensure continuity of character, plot, and visuals within one volume or across a comic-book series.) In such a session, writers and editors come up with as many ideas as they can, no matter how outlandish some might seem. They will then go back over the list of ideas and accept, reject, and refine them until they arrive at an agreed-upon list of workable stories. They will also determine if the story will be contained in one volume or if it will be a mini-series that continues across several volumes.

A writer who is not established with a comic-book publisher can also submit story ideas. He or she presents the idea in a *log line,* which is a one-line story summary, or in a lengthier *synopsis,* which is a one- or two-page summary of a story that contains the major events, some key lines of text, and brief descriptions of subplots. A synopsis is often the preferred method, as it provides more detail and makes it easier for artists to get a sense of how the action will unfold across the pages.

Space is at a premium in comics, so a writer must determine how to best convey the story, that is, how many panels will be used per page, and how many of those panels will contain text. There is no set limit to the number of panels than can appear on a page; in fact, the number of panels per page in one comic book usually varies. For example, a conversation between two people might take up 10 panels on one page, while a big action sequence might only require one or two panels. (The *splash page,* usually the first or second page in a comic book, is often rather elaborately drawn and thus consists of one panel.) The writer works closely with the comic-book artists when making these kinds of decisions.

Comic books writers employ two main forms of writing: *captions* and *dialogue.* Captions, which usually appear as boxes in the margins of a panel, are used to convey the passage of time ("Later that day . . ."), setting ("Meanwhile, back at the lab . . ."), and mood ("In the Golden Age of Planet Xon, even the sun shone brighter."). Dialogue generally appears in bubbles or balloons near the character that is speaking. These balloons may also show a character's internal thoughts, which are usually drawn differently to distinguish them from dialogue. A writer must handle dialogue carefully, as too many balloons on one page can confuse the reader. (The accepted rule of thumb is no more than three balloons per panel.)

A writer presents his or her story to an editor or artists in one of three ways: as a storyboard, as a script, or by writing text after the art has been created. In a storyboard, the writer makes a rough layout of the text and art by drawing crude comic-book panels with stick figures or basic art and the text in its proper place. This gives the artist a specific idea of how the action will unfold and how many panels the writer had in mind. When creating a comic-book script, a writer also does a panel-by-panel breakdown of the story and action, but uses only words to do so. For example, a comic-book script would contain pages labeled "Page 3-Panel 4" and "Page 3-Panel 5." Each page contains the clearly labeled captions, art directions, and dialogue for that panel.

In some instances the comic-book artist will draw all of the artwork for the book based on the writer's original synopsis. This works especially well in comics where action and plot are emphasized over dialogue and captions. In this scenario, once the panels have been drawn, the writer will create text that corresponds to the action.

Comic-book writers can be employed either as in-house staff or as freelancers. Pay varies according to experience and the position, but freelancers must provide their own office space and equipment such as computers and fax machines. Freelancers also are responsible for keeping tax records, sending out invoices, negotiating contracts, and providing their own health insurance.

REQUIREMENTS

High School

While in high school, build a broad educational foundation by taking courses in English, literature, foreign languages, history, general science, social studies, and computer science. Take art classes, as well, as these will help you understand the artistic skills and visual sense needed to create a comic book.

Postsecondary Training

Although obtaining a college degree is not required to become a comic-book writer, it may give you an advantage if you apply for a writing or editorial position in the small and competitive comic-book field. In addition, many comic-book writers cannot make a living in comic books alone and thus hold full-time positions in other writing and non-writing fields. Having a college degree will benefit you in this respect, as well. Many comic-book writers have a broad liberal arts background or majors in English, art, literature, history, philosophy, or social sciences. A number of schools offer courses in journalism, and some of them offer courses or majors in book publishing, publication management, and newspaper and magazine writing, which could be useful in preparing for work in this field.

Most comic-book publishers look for writers with proven writing experience. If you have served on high school or college newspapers, yearbooks, or literary magazines, or if you have worked for small community newspapers or radio stations, even in an unpaid position, you will be an attractive candidate. Many book publishers, magazines, newspapers, and radio and television stations have summer internship programs that provide valuable training in this regard. Interns do many simple tasks, such as running errands and answering phones, but some may be asked to perform research, conduct interviews, or even write some minor pieces.

Other Requirements

To be a comic-book writer, you should be creative and able to express ideas clearly, have a broad general knowledge and a good sense of visual and literary storytelling, be skilled in research techniques, and be computer literate. Other assets include curiosity, persistence, initiative, resourcefulness, an accurate memory, and, of course, a good knowledge of the different styles of comic books. As with most jobs that involve publishing, the ability to concentrate, work under pressure, and meet deadlines is essential for a comic-book writer.

EXPLORING

The best advice for a budding comic-book writer is to become as familiar with different styles of comics and stories as possible. Read about the history of comics, observing how they and the public's tastes in them have changed over the decades. See what types of stories were quick fads and which have stood the test of time. Read and reread different styles of comics and see how the writers have developed characters, mood, setting, and continuity across issues. Attend local and national comic-book conventions and talk to people working in the field. Ask how they got their start in the business and think about how you might go about getting your feet wet in this industry.

Most writers are also voracious readers. In addition to reading comic books, read novels, plays, memoirs, and biographies to learn the different ways in which writers handle character, plot, dialogue, and setting. Start to develop some of your own comic worlds, characters, and stories by fleshing out the details of each.

You can develop your sense of visual storytelling by visiting museums and seeing paintings that capture various actions, moods, and expressions. Practice storyboarding some of your own comic-book ideas to gain a sense of what works in the confines of the comic-book page and what does not.

Finally, you can test your interest and aptitude in the field of writing by serving as a reporter or writer on school newspapers, yearbooks, and literary magazines. Various writing courses and workshops will provide the opportunity to sharpen your writing skills.

EMPLOYERS

There are approximately 139,000 writers and authors currently employed in the United States, a small percentage of which are comic-book writers. Comic-book writers are employed by the two largest comic-book publishers, Marvel and DC, and by smaller comic publishers, book publishers who publish graphic novels, and humor and pop culture magazines. In many instances, comic-book writers make a living by working on a freelance or part-time basis for several of these types of publications.

Full-time writers also work for advertising agencies and public relations firms and work on journals and newsletters published by business and nonprofit organizations, such as professional associations, labor unions, and religious organizations. Other employers are government agencies and film production companies.

STARTING OUT

There is no one path to becoming a comic-book writer, but a fair amount of experience is required to gain a high-level position in the comic-book field. Some writers start out in entry-level positions at comic-book publishers as assistants or interns, which are sometimes unpaid positions. An assistant may at first be asked to sit in on brainstorming sessions to get a feel for how new ideas are decided upon. He or she may gradually be given more responsibility or input on new comic-book projects, which might include some writing responsibilities.

In many cases comic-book writers are simply comic fans who diligently submit their proposals and synopses to established comic-book publishers in the hopes of eventually getting an acceptance letter. Others pool resources with other talented friends and produce and distribute their own comic books with the hopes of eventually finding an audience. In any scenario, it is important to learn as much as possible about the workings of the comic-book industry and to form a substantial portfolio of ideas and writing samples. Showing that you can tackle various comic genres (such as action, horror, comedy, drama, romance, and science fiction) will showcase for publishers your creativity and versatility as a writer.

ADVANCEMENT

Many comic-book writers find their first jobs as interns or editorial or production assistants. Promotion into more responsible positions and full-scale writing responsibilities comes with diligence and experience.

Freelance or self-employed writers earn advancement in the form of larger fees as they gain exposure and establish their reputations.

EARNINGS

In 2003, median annual earnings for salaried writers and authors were $42,330 a year, according to the Bureau of Labor Statistics. The lowest 10 percent earned less than $22,090, while the highest 10 percent earned $87,390 or more. Freelancer comic-book writers may earn from $5,000 to $15,000 a year. Full-time established freelance comic-book writers may earn up to $75,000 a year.

WORK ENVIRONMENT

Working conditions for comic-book writers range from the comforts of home to a regular office environment, depending on whether the writer works full or part time and the type of comic-book publisher for which he or she works. A few of the larger comic-book publishers are housed in large offices in major U.S. cities, but most are modest operations that are located in small offices and, in some cases, in private homes. Many comic-book writers start their careers and build their portfolios by writing in their leisure time after work or school.

Comic-book writing, like all writing, can be arduous, but most writers are seldom bored. The most difficult element is the continual pressure of deadlines. People who are the most content as writers enjoy and work well with deadline pressure.

OUTLOOK

The employment of writers is expected to increase at an average rate through 2012, according to the U.S. Department of Labor. Competition for writing jobs has been and will continue to be keen, especially in the small and highly competitive field of comic books. The comic-book industry has seen many ups and downs over the past several decades, with the age and demographics of comic-book readers shifting to older, more discriminating audiences. Graphic novels and comics for older audiences are gaining popularity around the world, which has opened up more vistas for comic-book writers in terms of style and theme. Although finding work in the comic-book industry can be challenging, doing so is rewarding on many levels for the comic-book writer who displays creativity, versatility, and a true passion for the medium itself.

TO LEARN MORE ABOUT COMIC-BOOK WRITERS

BOOKS

Eisner, Will. *Comics & Sequential Art*. Poorhouse Press, 1985.

Gertler, Nat, ed. *Panel One: Comic Book Scripts by Top Writers*. Thousand Oaks, Calif: About Comics, 2002.

———. *Panel Two: More Comic Book Scripts by Top Writers*. Thousand Oaks, Calif: About Comics, 2005.

Haines, Lurene. *The Business of Comics: Everything a Comic Book Artist Needs to Make It in the Business*. New York: Watson-Guptill, 1998.

———. *The Writer's Guide to the Business of Comics*. New York: Watson-Guptill, 1998.

McCloud, Scott. *Understanding Comics.* Reprint ed. New York: HarperCollins, 1994.

Salisbury, Mark. *Writers on Comics Scriptwriting.* New York: Watson-Guptill, 2000.

ORGANIZATIONS AND WEBSITES

For the latest news in the comic-book industry and links to comics websites, visit the following sites:

Comic Book Industry Alliance

http://www.thecbia.com

Comic Book Resources

http://www.comicbookresources.com

TO LEARN MORE ABOUT STAN LEE

BOOKS

Benton, Mike. *The Comic Book in America: An Illustrated History*. Dallas, Tex.: Taylor, 1989.

Daniels, Les. *Marvel: Five Fabulous Decades of the World's Greatest Comics*. New York: Harry N. Abrams, 1993.

DeFalco, Tom. *Comic Creators on Spider-Man*. London, England: Titan, 2004.

Editors. *Current Biography Yearbook 1993*. Bronx, N.Y.: H. W. Wilson, 1993.

Fleischer, Michael L. *Encyclopedia of Comic Book Heroes*. New York: Macmillan, 1976.

Lee, Stan. *Bring on the Bad Guys*. New York: Simon & Schuster, 1976.

———. *Origin of Marvel Comics.* New York: Simon & Schuster, 1974.

———. *Secrets Behind the Comics.* New York: Famous Enterprises, 1947.

———. *Son of Origin of Marvel Comics.* New York: Simon & Schuster, 1975.

———. *The Superhero Women.* New York: Simon & Schuster, 1977.

Lee, Stan, and Bill Simon, Joe Everett, Jack Kirby. *Grandson of Origins of Marvel Comics.* New York: Marvel Entertainment, 1998.

Lee, Stan, and George Mair. *Excelsior! The Amazing Life of Stan Lee.* New York: Fireside/Simon & Schuster, 2002.

Lee, Stan, and John Buscema. *How to Draw Comics the Marvel Way.* New York: Simon & Schuster, 1978.

Raphael, Jordan, and Tom Spurgeon: *Stan Lee and the Rise and Fall of the American Comic Book.* Chicago: Chicago Review Press, 2003.

Robinson, Jerry. *The Comics: An Illustrated History of Comic Strip Art.* New York: Putnam, 1974.

Wright, Bradford W. *Comic Book Nation: The Transformation of Youth Culture in America.* Baltimore, Md.: John Hopkins University Press, 2001.

MAGAZINES

Sinclair, Tom. "Stan Lee: The Greatest Comic Book Writer in the World." *Entertainment Weekly*, May 20, 2003.

TELEVISION

A&E Biography: *Stan Lee* (1995)

History Channel: *Comic Book Heroes Unmasked* (2003)

WEBSITES

The following sites contain information on Stan Lee and the comic book industry in general:

The Big Cartoon Data Base

http://www.bcdb.com

The Comic Page

http://www.dereksantos.com/comicpage/index.html

Don Markstein's Toonopedia: Marvel Comics

http://www.toonopedia.com/marvel.htm

The History of Superhero Comic Books

http://www.geocities.com/Athens/8580/frames.html

Marvel Comics

http://www.marvel.com

Salon: Brilliant Careers: Stan Lee

http://www.salon.com/people/bc/1999/08/17/lee

INDEX

Page numbers in *italics* indicate illustrations.

ABOUT THE AUTHOR

James Robert Parish, a former entertainment reporter, publicist, and book series editor, is the author of numerous biographies and reference books of the entertainment industry including *Twyla Tharp: Choreographer*; *Denzel Washington: Actor*; *Halle Berry: Actor*; *Stephen King: Writer*; *Tom Hanks: Actor*; *Steven Spielberg: Filmmaker*; *The Hollywood Book of Scandal*; *Whitney Houston*; *The Hollywood Book of Love*; *Hollywood Divas*; *Hollywood Bad Boys*; *The Encyclopedia of Ethnic Groups in Hollywood*; *Jet Li*; *Jason Biggs*; *Gus Van Sant*; *The Hollywood Book of Death;* *Whoopi Goldberg*; *Rosie O'Donnell's Story*; *The Unofficial "Murder, She Wrote" Casebook*; *Today's Black Hollywood*; *Let's Talk! America's Favorite TV Talk Show Hosts*; *Black Action Pictures*; *Liza Minnelli*; *The Elvis Presley Scrapbook*; and *Hollywood's Great Love Teams.*

Mr. Parish is a frequent on-camera interviewee on cable and network TV for documentaries on the performing arts both in the United States and in the United Kingdom. Mr. Parish resides in Studio City, California.